A Parents' Guide to the
Internet

Jim McClellan

D1809274

Atlantic Books
London

First published in 2001 by Atlantic Books,
on behalf of Guardian Newspapers Ltd.

Atlantic Books is an imprint of
Grove Atlantic Ltd.

© Jim McClellan 2001

10 9 8 7 6 5 4 3 2 1

A CIP catalogue record for this book
is available from the British Library.

1 903809 24 X

Printed in Great Britain
by Clays Ltd, St Ives Plc

Designed by Bryony Newhouse

Grove Atlantic Ltd
29 Adam & Eve Mews
London W8 6UG

Contents

3 The next level

4 Essential clicks for kids

Introduction

Does the internet make it harder to be a parent? The American journalist Michael Lewis seems to think so. In *The Future Just Happened*, his recent BBC TV series about the cultural impact of the net, he argued that, because of the way it allows information to circulate more freely, the net threatens traditional authority figures. When he was plugging the series and the spin-off book, he told the *Guardian*: "There are some roles in society, like lawyers and doctors, where status revolves around having information others don't have. Parenthood is another one." Lewis went on to say that he didn't know much about what his lawyer father did all day at the office. Hence there was a mystique about him. Lewis won't enjoy that mystique with his own child, he reckons, because she'll have the net.

Now I like Lewis's work. *The New New Thing*, his book about the internet entrepreneur Jim Clark, is great. *The Future Just Happened* has lots of good stories too – about teenagers using the net to pass themselves off as lawyers and make hundreds of thousands of dollars trading shares. Lewis muses thoughtfully on the destabilizing cultural effects of the net. But when it comes to parents being undermined by the free-flowing info-economy of the online world, he does overstate things a little. He's not alone. Thinking that everything comes down to information is one of the big stupid ideas of the day, a fallacy that techno-types are particularly susceptible to. But being a parent is about more than merely having access to information that your kids don't. It's about having better judgement than they do. It's about exercising that judgement in their interest.

Of course, it isn't always easy to do that online. Let's flip that opening question around slightly. Is it harder to be a parent on the internet? Perhaps. To exercise your parental judgement online, you need the right information. You need to know how the net works. That's where this book comes in. The aim is to teach you what you need to know. The idea is to help you keep up with your kids when they get online, to help you keep them out of trouble and point them towards all the good stuff online. Telling you how to raise your kids isn't part of the plan, though. This isn't a parenting book – it's a net manual. Obviously, how you approach parenting is up to you. What this book aims to do is to give you the knowledge you need so you can do what you think is right for your kids on the net.

In *The Future Just Happened*, Lewis has interesting things to say about why teenagers in particular seem to embrace the net's possibilities in unexpected and challenging ways. In part, he suggests, it's because their identities are still fluid. They're still making themselves up, unlike their parents, who are usually rather set in their ways, distrustful of new (new) things and a little threatened by their kids' net skills. True enough, but there's another reason why kids can race ahead online. They have the time to learn about it, the time to try things out and see what happens. As a rule, parents don't. As a rule, you're lucky if you can manage an hour to yourself at the end of the day before you drift into unconsciousness. I'm a parent too. I know what it's like. So I've tried to make this book as easy to digest as possible. I've tried to avoid jargon and unnecessary detail. The idea is to get you online and up to speed as quickly and painlessly as possible.

1 **Getting connected** offers advice on the hardware and software you need and goes on to discuss choosing an internet service provider (ISP) and connecting for the first time.

2 **Getting to grips with the net** takes you through the most popular net activities. It covers browsing the web, searching for information, downloading software, accessing online multimedia, using email, discussion groups, chatrooms and instant messaging.

3 **The next level** gives you advice on shopping on the net, putting up a personal homepage and fast, broadband connections. Along the way, I've tried to suggest how a particular net activity might benefit your family. I've also tried to point out various problems parents should look out for with each activity.

4 **Essential clicks for kids** points you in the direction of some of the best websites for children. Alongside a basic directory of educational/entertainment sites, you'll find specific information on kids' online directories and lists of sites for preschoolers and teenagers.

5 **Protecting your kids online** tells you the things you need to worry about online, as far as your kids are concerned, and advises you on the best way to keep your children out of trouble.

6 **Essential clicks for parents** is a directory for you. You'll find lots of useful advice about parenting online and you can swap ideas and get support from other parents – if you know where to look. This section tells you.

Finally, at the back of the book you'll find information about UK internet service providers, a glossary of techno-jargon and some suggestions for further reading about the net. I've tried to structure this guide so that, whatever stage you're at with the net, you'll get something useful out of it.

• If you don't yet have a computer, start at the beginning. If you have a computer, but no connection to the net, go to Section 1, page 12, where you'll find advice on how to hook it up to the net.

- If you have an older computer you're planning to use, there are guidelines that should help you decide whether it's up to the job on page 21.

- If you have a reasonably new computer with an internal modem, but you've never bothered to get connected, head for Section 1, page 23, where you'll find tips on setting up a deal with an Internet Service Provider and connecting for the first time.

- If you have a computer that's connected to the net and you've been online, but never really got into it, go to section 2, where you'll find clear and concise 'how to' information about all the basic net activities and more. Incidentally, even if you're already online, you might find it useful to check the advice about choosing ISPs on page 26, just to make sure you have the best deal for your family.

- If you're comfortable with the net, start at section 3, where you'll find some specific advice about what to do there with your kids. However, even if you know the net, you might find Section 2 useful, since I've tried to point out potential problems that might arise with different aspects of the net.

In the end, of course, how you read this book is up to you. But please don't think you have to read the whole lot before you get online. Throughout the book you will see various Alerts – captions boxed-off from the main text with this icon *(!)*, featuring useful bits of information. The idea with these is to offer bits of advice that might come in handy, unscramble some of the more forbidding pieces of techno-speak and point you towards web sites where you can find out more about a particular subject. Incidentally, if you do come across a piece of netspeak that isn't explained in an Alert box, turn to page 307, where you'll find a glossary of internet-related terminology. Before you get started, though, here are a few initial tips:

- **Don't be scared of the net**
  Self-induced technophobia can be one of the biggest problems people face when dealing with the net. It's true that getting online is still harder than it should be, but it's nowhere near as hard as it used to be. If you know how to use a PC running Windows or an Apple Mac, you will crack the net, no problem.

- **Don't believe all the scare stories about the net**
  The net is not heaving with paedophiles, and pornography will not leap out at your children as soon as they log on. True, there is a lot of porn online and some of it can find its way onto your screen unbidden. But there are things you can do to stop that. It's also true that it's potentially easy for children to access sites featuring all sorts of unsuitable material – not just porn. But again, there are things you can do to protect them. As for paedophiles – yes, there are some online. In some ways, the net makes it easier for them to get on to your children's computer screens. But most get no further than that – the computer screen. In a few sad cases, things spill over into the real world. But this usually happens because parents have no idea what is happening, because they leave their kids to use the net unsupervised. You can't do that. You have to be an active parent where the net is concerned. But you know that already. Presumably that's why you bought this book. And you'll find tips on how to protect your children from cyber-predators on page 267. The dangers paedophiles pose online has been much discussed, so much so that some parents feel rather powerless when it comes to protecting their children. Don't feel that way. There's plenty you can do to protect your children on the net.

- **Don't overvalue the net**
  Learning about the net will obviously help your children when it comes to school and work. But don't force your kids on to the net

before they're ready. Younger children will probably get more from multimedia CD-ROMs than from the net, which is really for older kids who can read. Of course, most kids won't need forcing – you'll have to drag them from their PCs kicking and screaming. Given the hype surrounding the net, you may be tempted to assume that two hours online are necessarily better for your kids than two hours watching TV. Don't. You need to limit your kids' net time in the same way you try to limit their TV time. Help them find a balance between the net and the real world. And don't use the net as an electronic child minder. You need to be involved in what they do online. That doesn't mean you need to sit with them all the time while they're on the net. But you can't just switch off when they log on.

- **Talk to your kids about what they do on the net. Be prepared to learn from them**
  Don't treat the net as a kids' thing, something you leave to them. Talk to your kids about what they do online. Make sure they know they can talk to you if they come across something on the net that upsets or scares them. If they're already online and surfing like pros, while you're still getting started, why not ask for their advice. Let them take the lead and show you round the net. You could learn something useful, plus it will make the net a conversational subject between you, something you share, rather than a private world your child retreats into, away from you.

- **The things you teach your kids to help them stay safe in the real world also work online**
  The net is a new technology, whose uses are still being worked out. But that doesn't mean that real-world knowledge isn't useful when you're online. When you're net shopping, you need to know some new things about protecting your credit card data. But the shopping know-how you use on the high street will also come

in handy. Similarly, with parenting online, you need to know about the new things that the net makes possible. But what you already know from looking out for your kids in the real world will also come in handy. Be wary of strangers. Don't give out personal information. Respect other people. All are important lessons your kids should heed when they use the net.

- **Make sure the family PC is set up in a shared family location**
  Keeping your kids safe online can involve learning how to work bits of software that create technological barriers and filters. But it also involves setting boundaries in the real world, creating guidelines and agreements about how much time your kids can spend online, what they can and can't do there and what they should do if things go wrong or turn nasty. One of the best things you can do to head off possible problems for your kids online is to think about where you put the family PC. Make sure you put it a communal space – the lounge or kitchen – and not in a child's bedroom. If your computer is in a communal space, you can keep an eye on them. Even if you're not there, the fact that you might walk in at any moment may make them think a little harder about getting up to something. By putting it in a communal space, you also make the point that the computer is a family machine and not your child's to do with as they wish.

Where you put the computer might not seem like much. But believe me – lots of parents have found that it helps. Whether you do or not, please feel free to drop me a line at **jim.mcclellan@guardian.co.uk**. We're all still learning how the net works, both for us and for our kids. If you discover something you think might benefit other parents, tell me about it and I'll include it in any future updates. Incidentally, there are bound to be a few errors in the book you're about to read, if only because things are constantly changing on the net. New bits of software appear out of nowhere and take the net by storm; web sites go out of business and offline. If you find something that's wrong – an address that doesn't seem to work, for example – drop me a line and I'll do my best to point you in the right direction.

By the way, once you get comfortable with the web, you can read more about Michael Lewis and his theories about the net's cultural effects, if you feel like it.

- The *Guardian's* interview with Michael Lewis is at
  http://www.guardian.co.uk/Archive/Article/0,4273,4224196,00.html.
- The web site for the BBC2 series, *The Future Just Happened*, is at
  http://news.bbc.co.uk/hi/english/static/in_depth/programmes/2001/future/default.stm.
- His fascinating story about Jonathan Lebed, the fifteen-year-old who made hundreds of thousands of dollars trading stocks online (illegally according to the US financial authorities, but not according to Lewis) should still be on the *New York Times* web site at
  http://www.nytimes.com/2001/02/25/magazine/25STOCK-TRADER.html.
- Ditto his story about Marcus Arnold, another fifteen-year-old who managed, with no legal experience, to convince users of a popular 'expert' site that he was a top lawyer, at
  http://www.nytimes.com/2001/07/15/magazine/15INTERNET.html.

A word of warning – the web addresses given above end in full stops. That's simply because they happen to come at the end of the relevant sentences. Web addresses as such, however, don't end in full stops: if you add one to a particular address, it won't work. We'll cover this later, in more detail, but I thought it wouldn't hurt to mention it now. Incidentally, you'll need to register with the *New York Times* to access their sites. But at the time of writing, that was still free. Isn't the net great?

1
Getting connected

To get online, you need hardware, software, a connection to the net and an account with a company that can provide you with net access. Getting all these things is a relatively pain-free process these days, though if you're starting from scratch, that is, if you live in a completely computer-free home, you will have to spend a fair amount of money before you can get online.

Hardware

In theory, you don't have to rely on a personal computer to access the net. You can also use personal digital assistants (aka PDAs), pocket PCs, mobile phones, TVs fitted with special set-top boxes, games consoles and internet appliances designed for the sole purpose of getting you online. However, the standard personal computer is still your best bet, especially if you're buying for your family. Why?

- A PC is a multi-purpose machine – you can use it write documents, crunch numbers and play games as well as surfing the net.

- Your kids can use it while you watch TV – or vice-versa.

- A PC can't easily be carted off into a child's bedroom – an important concern, as you'll soon discover.

- Entry-level PCs now make the net relatively easy. Both PCs running Windows and Apple Macs now come with everything you need to get online, from internal modems to pre-installed connection software.

- The price of both PCs and Macs has also dropped over the last few years. They're still not cheap. But the days of spending well over £1,000 to get started online have gone.

- Mobile devices are aimed at business users and only offer a limited version of the net – email retrieval and very stripped-down web browsing on a tiny screen.

Set-top boxes may look like a cheaper way to get started online. But personally, I'm not that sold on the idea of checking out webpages and doing my email via the TV.

- TV monitors aren't best suited to delivering legible text (and there's still an awful lot of text online).

- Watching TV and wandering round the net are two very different experiences. TV is more passive and the net is more active. With the latter, you need to be up close to the screen, figuring out what to do and where to go next.

- It's not easy writing email perched on the couch pecking away at a cross between a TV remote control and a miniature keyboard.

- And what happens when you want to watch TV and your kids want to get online, or vice versa?

There's a theory that video game consoles will, over the next few years, become the net-connected set-top box of choice. You can already get online via Sega's Dreamcast machine. Sony's Playstation 2 and Microsoft's upcoming X-Box will offer something similar in the future. All very interesting. But for now, you should buy a games console to play games. If you want to try out the net with it, fine. But be prepared for a rather underwhelming experience. Don't expect the flexibility and choice, in terms of software and access, that you get with other devices. And be aware that you will buying something that is seen more as your child's device than as a family resource. This may cause problems later when it comes to keeping an eye on what your kids do online.

Modems

Here's the bad news. A computer isn't the only piece of hardware you need to get online. You also need a modem, which will convert the digital information your computer works with into audio signals that can then be sent down a standard telephone line. (The name's a compression of the technical term Modulator Demodulator, by the way.) Here's the good news: virtually all new PCs and Macs now come with internal modems as standard.

If you already have a computer that doesn't have something suitable installed, you can buy an external modem. You connect this to your computer via one of the serial ports at the back of your machine. External modems usually need to be plugged into the mains (unless they're USB devices set up to run off the power source your computer uses). They're easier to replace if they go wrong or you buy something newer and faster. Of course, if you're really technically minded, you can always buy an internal modem and open up your machine and install it yourself.

Modem speed

The speed at which a modem can send and receive information is measured in bits per second (bps). The higher the speed, the faster data gets sent back and forth between you and the net. Is speed important? Yes, but... Sometimes things are just slow online and it's nothing to do with your connection. Whatever you get, you'll wish you had something faster. If you're using an old modem, the absolute minimum speed you should put up with is 28.8Kbps (which means data gets sent at 28,800 bits per second). Nowadays 56.6Kbps modems are standard. For various technical reasons, they receive data at 56.6Kbps but send it back at 36.6Kbps. In addition, only in ideal conditions will they receive data at 56.6Kbps. Most of the time they'll chug along at something between 40 and 50Kbps.

Modem advice If you have trouble with your modem or need advice about upgrading, have a look at Modem Help
http://www.modemhelp.com.

Buying a computer

Handing over a large amount of money can be rather daunting. Here's some advice to help the process go as smoothly as possible.

Do your research

Obviously. But if you are going to spend between £500 and £1,000, it's worth taking your time and finding out what's available.

- The consumer computer magazines are a good place to start – the ads as well as the editorial. It's the quickest way to get an idea of what you'll get for your money.

- It's easy to buy direct from the various computer manufacturers: you can specify exactly what you want and get a pretty good price. But if you're not familiar with computers, you may want to actually play around with different machines to see which suits you best. So it may be worth making a trip to your nearest computer superstore – even if you don't plan on actually buying there.

- Think a bit about what you and your kids plan to do with your computer, aside from the net. If your children are over ten, it may be worth investing in a machine with a reasonably fast processor, a sizeable hard disk, lots of RAM (Random Access Memory) and special graphics cards, so that they can play the latest games. If your children are under ten, you might be able to get away with a less powerful machine for the moment.

Things change all the time in the computing world, and by the time you read this, the technical specs for the average entry-level computer will no doubt be completely different. But, at the time of writing:

- £700 (including VAT) bought you a reputable name-brand PC with a 900MHz processor, 128MB of RAM, a 20GB hard drive, a 17" monitor, a CD-ROM, speakers, modem and a lot more. This is more than adequate for most online activities.

- £950 (including VAT) bought you a powerful name-brand PC with a 1.5 GHz processor, 128MB of RAM, a 40GB hard drive, 17" monitor, a 32MB graphics/video card, a combined DVD/CD-RW drive (the CD-RW lets you make or 'burn' your own CDs), modem, sound card, speakers, software and more. This kind of system is more than adequate for the net and should keep game-crazy teens happy for a few years as well.

As for Macs, at the time of writing:

- £680 got you an entry-level iMac with a 500MHz processor, 64MB of RAM, 20GB hard drive, modem, CD-ROM, an 8MB graphics card and lots more. This is fine for most people's net use.

- £1000 bought you a faster iMac, with a 600MHz processor, 256MB of RAM, 40GB hard drive, a CD-RW drive, modem, graphics cards, software and more. This is fine for the net and good if you want to mess around editing video and making your own little films on the computer.

Mac or PC?

Which should you go for – an Apple Macintosh or an IBM-compatible PC running Microsoft Windows? (OK – there are other options but they're mainly for geeks.) This remains one of the great ideological divides in computer culture. That said, many of the differences between the two machines are less marked than they used to be. It's now as easy to set up a new PC as it is a Mac. In the past, the net was quite a PC-centric place. ISPs seemed happier dealing with PC users. But that's changed now. And though the bulk of new net software does tend to come out first for the PC, it's pretty easy to find Mac versions of the software you need for the net. Here are a few things to think about when you're trying to decide:

- Swapping files with friends is generally easier if you have the same sort of computer as them. If you want to bring work home from the office, it helps to run the same sort of computer as your workplace. That generally means a computer running Windows (Microsoft has over 90 per cent of the PC market). That said, mainstream programs like Word come in both flavours and can read documents created in the competing version.

- If you want a user-friendly computer, some sort of Apple Mac is still usually the best bet – though PCs have got a lot better recently.

- The Mac is also still the choice of many creative professionals – artists, journalists and designers. If that's what you do (or hope to do in the future), the Mac is probably what you want.

- Remember – you're buying a family machine. There's a larger selection of games and multimedia software available for the PC.

Covering yourself

Obviously, you want the PC you buy to last a long time. You want it to be able to cope with the various demands your kids will place on it. So what should you do?

- Whatever computer you buy, it's usually worth spending money on extending guarantees or service warranties, so long as you don't end up paying through the nose for them. Computers remain unreliable machines.

- Check out the companies behind the deals on offer in the computer magazines. You want reliability from your PC. You want to be able to take it back to the manufacturers if problems occur (or at least give them a call). Some of the companies offering those great prices look like they might not be around that long.

- Think about what computer types call future-proofing. If you can afford it, think about spending a bit more money on a mid-range machine that will have enough power to handle the software that comes out the year after you bought it. Of course, most of us make do with the software that comes with our new PC. We don't buy new stuff every year. That said, it is nice to feel that the machine you bought a few months ago hasn't already been dismissed as an antique by the industry.

- If you do have the money to 'future-proof', you should try to get extra RAM, a faster processor and a bigger hard drive. More RAM will make your system run more smoothly and help when you want to run more than one application at once. Processor speed will come in handy if your kids are fans of cutting-edge games. As for hard drives, although they seem huge now, compared to what was on offer a few years ago, you'll be surprised how quickly you can fill them up.

Other options

You don't have to drag yourself down to the high street and buy a bog-standard PC. There are other options.

- **A laptop** A new one will come with everything you need. But it will be more expensive than an equivalent PC. Also, as I mentioned earlier, one way to maintain control over what your

children do online is to put your PC in a family location – the
lounge, or the kitchen, for example. If you buy a laptop and your
child has a telephone point in their bedroom, it will be easy for
them to get online away from your watchful eyes.

- **A second-hand computer** The computer world is full of speed
  junkies who sell off perfectly good machines so they can get the
  latest, fastest thing. So you may find a real bargain. But before you
  buy, get a computer-literate friend to look it over, so you don't get
  conned.

Using an older PC/Mac

Perhaps you bought a computer a few years back to do the odd
bit of word-processing. Will it get you and your kids online? It
depends. If you're happy with reading and writing text and
don't want multimedia, you can get by online with a very
low tech, low spec computer. But I really wouldn't advise it.
Struggling along with this will be very, very tiresome. And
you'll only be getting half the net. Worse, it will be the half that
your kids aren't that keen on. So as well as struggling with your
machine, you'll have to put up with a lot of whining.

If you're using an old machine and want to see a bit more of
what's on offer online, the minimum requirements are:

- **RAM** You can get by with 32MB (though 64MB will make the
  latest web browsers run a lot quicker).

- **Hard disk** Once online you might download a lot of software.
  Realistically you'll need at least a 2-3GB hard disk – though something bigger would be preferable.

- **Multimedia** To listen to music or watch video clips online, you need a decent soundcard and speakers, a video card with a few megabytes of video RAM and graphics accelerators.

- **Processor speed** Not as much of an issue as some make out, but a reasonably quick processor (400MHz, for instance) won't hurt.

- **Monitors Size** is up to you. If you're going to use a creaky old PC, check that your monitor has at least 256 colours.

- **Operating systems** Though you can, in theory, get by with a computer that runs an old operating system (i.e. Windows 3.x), everything becomes that bit more fiddly. You have to get separate bits of software for different tasks. Windows 95/98 and NT have the programs you need to get online already built into them. The same goes for Macs from System 7.5 on.

- **CD-ROM drive** If you are running an ancient computer which doesn't have a CD ROM drive, getting software on floppy discs will be a real problem.

- **Modem** You can get by with a 28.8K modem, but something that runs at 56.6K will make your life online a lot easier. 14.4K modems are much too slow for the web these days.

If your computer doesn't quite fit the bill, you could try upgrading it yourself. Inserting extra chunks of RAM into a PC is actually pretty easy. But if you're a computer innocent, the idea of fiddling with computer innards will undoubtedly seem a little daunting. You can get people to do it for you, though by the time you've paid for them and the extra components, you might find you could have bought a new machine for the same money.

Your connection

You have your computer and modem. The next thing you need is a connection to the net. The best bet for the beginner is the telephone line. It's simple and just about everyone's got one. All you need to do is plug in your modem jack and you can get started. There are things you can do to make things go a little smoother before you get started:

- Disable Call Waiting if you have it. Otherwise it may break into your net calls and cut you off.

- You may experience problems if you've set your telephone up to withhold Caller Line Identification (CLI), information that is forwarded with calls made from BT residential lines (it helps the 1471 function work). You can remove this on a call-by-call basis, though it is a bit fiddly: basically, you need to get your net dial-up software to add 1470 at the start of your net account number.

- BT's Call Minder (or similar services offered by other providers) can be useful. This takes voice messages while your line is engaged, then calls you afterwards to tell you that you have voice-mail. If your kids are online a lot, this can become rather useful.

- Look at the latest pricing offers from your service provider. If you're with BT, put your ISP's number on your Family and Friends list or make it your Best Friend number. You will save a bit of money. Not much, admittedly, but every bit helps.

Internet Service Providers (ISPs)

Your computer is hooked up to your modem, which is plugged into your phone line. Next you need to dial up an internet service provider, or ISP, who will provide you with a connection to the net. ISPs have changed an awful lot over the last few years. Things certainly aren't perfect yet, but in general, ISPs have become more business-like, more reliable and user-friendly – and, yes, cheaper. The two types of ISP you should think about using are:

- Free ISPs, which offer net access for free. However, you still pay your telephone charges. These can add up if you or your kids spend a long time on the net.

- ISPs offering so-called unmetered access deals, in which you pay a flat monthly fee that covers both net access and your telephone bills – so you can stay online as long as you like (in theory).

Many of the big name ISPs offer both sorts of deal. Incidentally, AOL is, strictly speaking, an online service, in that, apart from net access, it also offers various services (in particular its chatrooms) that are only available to its subscribers. In the early days of the net, there were a few online services. Now AOL and Compuserve (aimed more at business users) are the only survivors.

Choosing an ISP – the quick way

So which is the right ISP (and the right ISP deal) for you and your kids? It all depends on how much you end up using the net, on how old your kids are, when they want to get online and what they like doing when they're there. The best way to find all these things out is to just get online for a month or so and try things out. Don't worry too much about your telephone bills. Instead, concentrate on figuring out what you like about the net. Then you'll be in a position to make some real decisions. So, if you're just starting out, don't waste time researching ISPs. Instead, just pick up a disc from one of the better known free ISPs or one of the free trial offers from big companies like AOL, and just do it, as it were.

So where do you get the software you need?

- A new computer will probably come with software from some of the bigger ISPs pre-installed.

- Call some ISPs and ask for one of their trial discs. You'll find a list of telephone numbers for some of the better known operations on page 305.

- Buy one of the big net magazines – Future Publishing's *.net* and Emap's *Internet Magazine* are probably the two best known. Often they come with discs from some of the big ISPs. They also feature extensive lists of all the ISPs currently operating in the UK (plus contact details).

- You can also pick up discs for the free ISPs on your local High Street. Freeserve discs are given away at branches of Dixons. You can get Tesco's discs at Tesco supermarkets and WH Smith discs from WH Smith, obviously. Woolworths usually have the Netscape Online discs.

Once you've got the software you need, go to page 33, where you'll find some tips on connecting for the first time. Then once you've been online for a while, come back to the following section.

Free trials that cost In the past, there have been problems with ISP free trials. People have found it hard to unsubscribe and have wound up being charged by the ISP as if they had actually signed up. So, if you do use a free trial disc, let the ISP concerned know promptly if you don't want to continue, and check your credit card bills carefully to make sure they don't charge you.

Choosing an ISP – the painstaking way

Some people love researching and pondering their product choices. And there is plenty to ponder when picking an ISP. It might help to ask your friends which ISP they use and what they think of them. Then again, perhaps not. Moaning about your ISP is standard among net-users. Instead, buy one of the net magazines. Both *Internet Magazine* and *.net* run regular looks at ISP performance. *Internet Magazine* is particularly useful here. It regularly rates all the major ISPs, using a series of tests that check how easy it is to connect and how fast those connections are. Results are given for last month's performance. But there's also a chart showing performance over the last half-year, which is useful. New ISPs can often start well, then slip down the charts as they become overwhelmed with traffic.

Comparing ISPs

There are a few basics that all ISPs now provide. They all let you connect via a local call. All of them give you the software you need, though their interpretation of that usually means a web browser and nothing else. Beyond that, the things on offer do vary a little. For most people, the most important thing to think about when you're trying to pick an ISP is cost – there's some detailed advice on that in the following section.

Here's a few of the things you should think about.

• **Email** Most ISPs give you your own email account, usually what's known as a POP3 mail account – though some still try to get you to make do with a free web email service – for example a Hotmail account. With the latter, you have to visit a web site to pick up/read your email. This makes it very easy to pick up your mail when you're away from your own computer. That said, most people like to have a POP3 account and a webmail account as well. It's up to you. Most ISPs, but not all, will give you unlimited email addresses on the same account – useful for families, since each family member can have their own personal address.

> **POP3**   POP3, as in POP3 mail, stands for Post Office Protocol, version 3. This is the protocol that is used when it comes to receiving email. SMTP (aka Simple Mail Transfer Protocol) is used to send email. POP3 is pretty much the standard and helps you pick up your mail while you're travelling.

- **Content** Most ISPs have a homepage that features news, community areas, chatrooms, shopping services, search engines and much else. Generally you don't have to sign up with a service to access their homepage, though there are exceptions. You do need to sign up to AOL to access its chatrooms and information services.

- **Family services** Some ISPs sell themselves as family-friendly. They supply free filtering software and often their conferences and chatrooms are moderated, which means, in theory, that there's someone around to keep order and deal with online pests. AOL has its own controls that parents can use to protect their children from some of the dodgier things online.

- **Support** Some ISPs charge up to £1 a minute if you call them for help. Some offer free support calls while you're getting started. Some offer free support all the time. Many ISPs have made connecting so easy that you often don't need much help. That said, it may be an issue for you. In addition, find out when the telephone support lines are open.

- **Track record** Look into the background and history of the ISP you're thinking of using – try the *Internet Magazine* survey mentioned above. A big high street name won't necessarily be any better at net access than someone you've never heard of.

- **Access** You don't want to sign up to an ISP, then discover that you can't actually get online because the lines are always engaged at peak time, or that when you do connect, things move incredibly slowly because the ISP is over-subscribed and can't cope with the traffic. So call and make some inquiries. Ask about their subscriber-to-modem ratio. People say you should be looking for something around 15 to 1.

- **Web space** Virtually all ISPs offer you space online where you and your kids can put up personal webpages. The amount of space varies. Most assume that you'll treat it as a bit of fun. If you get serious, you may find yourself having to pay the ISP for hosting your pages. Incidentally, if you do put up a page and it becomes 'too popular', your ISP can cut it off. You might want to check their policy on this.

- **User names and domain names** Some ISPs let you pick your own user name/screen name/nickname – i.e. the name that appears at the start of your email address – the **jim** part of **jim@anotherISP.net**. Some don't, in which case find out the name you'll be stuck with.

- **Spam, advertising and viruses** Many ISPs take action to try to stop spam before it gets into your mailbox. Others will offer advice and, in some cases, spam-filtering software. Spam can be very irritating, so find out what an ISP does to stop it. A few ISPs cover their costs by pumping ads at their users while they surf. This bothers some users – others just filter it out. Some ISPs also offer free virus-checking programs.

Spam Net slang for unsolicited email sent in bulk to thousands of users at once, i.e. electronic junk mail. It's also a verb – you can spam someone as well as receive spam. The name comes from the *Monty Python* sketch and is supposed to refer to the way it keeps on coming.

- **Newsgroups** Some newer ISPs don't bother with the rather anarchic online discussion groups known as Usenet newsgroups, figuring perhaps that they belong to the old geeky net. Some newsgroups carry material that is illegal/pornographic. But many newsgroups are thriving communities where like-minded adults can swap ideas. They may not be suitable for your kids, but you might enjoy them. Talk to an ISP about which newsgroups they carry, whether they block the dodgier ones and whether they can help keep your kids away from the unsuitable groups.

- **Old PCs** If you have a PC running Windows 3.x or a pre system 7.5 Mac, you will also need a TCP/IP stack to get online. A TCP/IP stack is several bits of software in one (TCP/IP software, packet driver software and sockets software), each of which is needed in order to send and receive data across the net. Many ISPs now live in a post-Windows 95 world and so may not be able to help you here.

TCP/IP As mentioned before, TCP stands for Transmission Control Protocol. IP stands for Internet Protocol. Both 'protocols' (think of them as standard networking languages) allow your computer to communicate with the internet.

Incidentally, if you do call a prospective ISP to ask about any of the above, the way they deal with your queries will tell you something about them. How long does it take to get a few answers? How helpful are they? Do you get stuck on hold? And if you do order software, how long does it take to arrive? If your call meets with an unhelpful response and the software is slow to turn up, it's as good an indication as any that their net access service may not be quite up to scratch.

....
Cutting the cost of getting online
....

Ideally, you want to get fast reliable access for the lowest possible price. This doesn't necessarily mean the cheapest unmetered deal currently on offer. There's always a trade-off to be made.

- Often the companies offering the lowest price draw huge levels of traffic, can't cope and provide slow access.

- An unmetered deal may not be right for you if you or your kids don't use the net that much.

- Be careful, though. It's easy to lose track of time online and wind up with a serious phone bill. Lots of things on the net – from chatting and shopping to downloading media files and free software programs – do take time.

- It's nice to be a bit more relaxed while you're online, rather than always worrying about how much money it's costing you.

So which kind of deal will save you the most money?
Go for a free ISP and pay your telephone bills:

- If your children are still quite young – under eight, say – and you only take them online every now and then.

- If you only use the net for email and the occasional browse, and connect mainly during the evening or at weekends, for less than an hour each day.

Go for some sort of unmetered deal:

- If your children are a bit older and are starting to use the net for schoolwork and fun

- If your children are teenagers who like to chat online.

If you do choose an unmetered deal, there are several things you should consider.

- Most unmetered deals cost somewhere between £12 and £15 a month. It's not always the most sensible thing to go for the ISP offering the cheapest flat rate. It might be better to pay a little more for faster, reliable access.

- Some unmetered deals only offer free calls to an internet connection in the evenings or at weekends. If your kids get online when they get home from school – and they will – you'll get a serious telephone bill.

- Are there any strings attached to the price? Some ISPs ask for a joining fee as well as the monthly payments. Some charge an annual fee instead of a monthly rate. Others make you change your telecoms provider.

- Check the terms and conditions before you sign up. Most ISPs reserve the right to throw you off the service if you abuse it. However, abuse is defined in rather interesting ways on some services. In the past, some unmetered services outlawed things teenagers love – like instant messaging, online gaming and net radio stations.

- If you can't connect easily at peak times and if, when you do, things move slowly, you should be able to change to someone who can do better. Easier said than done, if you're committed to a year-long deal. So always balance flexibility against cost.

Things are still changing in the unmetered access business. So the first thing you need to do is get some up-to-date information.

- Buy the net magazines to see what they have to say about current unmetered deals.

- Go to Net4Nowt **http://www.net4nowt.com** or ISP Review **http://www.ispreview.co.uk** for the latest news and reviews.

- *.net* magazine runs a forum where readers can compare ISP experiences. Go to **http://www.futureforums.co.uk/netmag/default.asp** and look for the relevant link.

Connecting for the first time

Connecting to the net for the first time back in the early nineties was hard work. An early subscriber to Demon, the UK's first ISP, apparently commented that setting up an account and connecting was 'a bit like giving birth – so difficult that afterwards, you can never quite remember how you did it'. (This comes from *net.wars*, Wendy Grossman's enjoyable book about net culture.) Things are a lot easier now. Many ISPs now go out of their way to help out nervous newcomers. Of course, attempting anything for the first time is always a little disconcerting. But don't worry – it won't be that bad.

Installing an external modem

If you buy a new computer, it will more than likely come with a pre-installed modem. If you do need to install your own external modem, here's how:

1 Plug your modem up to your computer, turn it on, then turn on your computer. Often your computer will detect your new modem and then ask you to insert the special installation disc it came with.

2 If that doesn't happen, if you're running Windows 95/98, click the *START* button, then select *SETTINGS*, then *CONTROL PANEL*, then double-click on the *MODEMS* icon. You'll then be walked through the installation process and prompted to insert the disk. Then it's just a question of specifying the modem you're using from a list of possibilities.

3 If you need to change the settings, click on the *PROPERTIES* button. The only thing you really need to worry about here is connection speed. Always pick a speed well above that officially listed for your modem, preferably double.

....

The connection

....

Most ISPs now provide introductory packages that walk you through the installation and configuration process and make the first connection for you, setting up your account automatically. All you have to do is put one of their discs in your computer and follow the instructions. They all work slightly differently, but they're all roughly the same, if you see what I mean.

1 Once the disc has started, you may have to enter some information about your system – whether you're using Windows 95 or 98 or some version of the Mac OS (Operating System).

2 Then you click on a *REGISTER* button and the disc will use your computer's internet connection package to dial up the ISP. You'll usually go to a registration form. To fill it out, just click in the relevant boxes.

3 At this point, you'll pick a password and confirm it. As usual, with passwords, don't pick something obvious. Go for a combination of words and letters.

4 You'll also be given the chance to choose your screen name/email name – i.e. the name that will go at the start of your mail address at the ISP (as in **jim@anotherisp.net**).

5 Free trial discs from AOL and other ISPs usally have a number / password on them which you have to enter at some point. You also have to give your credit card details – part of the security procedures to make sure that you don't keep trying to log on for free with trial discs. You shouldn't be charged, unless you decide to sign up at the end of the trial period. However, some companies have had problems here. So check your next credit-card bill.

6 Look out for something about the ISP sending you email about all their wonderful projects. It's up to you, but I prefer not to get too much of this kind of stuff. So make sure the relevant box is ticked or unticked as necessary.

7 Once the form is sent, you usually get a message confirming the details you entered. Often you get something telling you that your nickname/email name has already gone and you have to come up with something else. From here you can click on your browser and you're ready to go.

> **Choosing screen names** When it comes to picking a screen name, women should pick something that doesn't identify them as female, if they want to avoid potential hassles. If you give children their own account/screen name, make sure they pick something non-gender specific. Names that focus around colours and interests are good.

Sometimes, once the set up process is done, you'll be disconnected. You can then connect properly by starting your browser.

1 Click on the browser icon on your desktop. That will also start up your browser and the connection file created on your disc by the ISP.

2 Once your connection software is running, you'll hear the modem open the telephone line and tap out a number. If your ISP isn't engaged, you'll hear chirruping fax-like noises as your modem establishes a connection.

3 Onscreen, you'll see a dialog box that tells you what's happening – when your computer is dialing and when it's verifying your password.

4 Once you're connected, a dialog box will appear telling you you're online. This usually has a *DISCONNECT* button you can use to log off. It also keeps tabs on how long you spend online.

5 Your browser will then load its homepage. It will usually be something put up by your ISP.

Congratulations –you're online. Now it's just a matter of deciding where you want to go or what you want to do.

ISP user directories and profiles Some ISPs put some of the information you give them when you set up an account into a contacts directory of their users. If you want to protect your privacy (and avoid junk mail), make sure you opt out from this. Make sure that, if you create an account for your child, they're not added to any publicly accessible directory and identified as a child. Many ISPs let you create a personal profile, which details who you are, what you like and so on. Kids love putting these together. Make sure they don't give away any important information if they do create one of these. Details of hobbies, favourite bands etc. are fine. Real world addresses (home or school), email addresses and telephone numbers are not.

Connecting with an older computer

Getting online for the first time is usually hassle-free these days, unless you're using an older computer. To connect to the net, you need something called a TCP/IP stack. If your computer runs Windows 95/98, Windows NT or Macintosh System 7.5 (and anything after that), then you already have something suitable. Your ISP's introductory package will work with the TCP/IP stack already on your machine. When you install it, it will create a connection file that it will then use each time you call up your ISP. However, if you're running Windows 3.x, you will need to install a TCP/IP stack. Your ISP should have sent you what you need – probably a version of Trumpet Winsock. If you have an older Macintosh, you'll need MacTCP/MacPPP. Contact your ISP about this.

Manually configuring your connection

Even though modern ISP software usually sets up your connection for you, you may still have to manually configure your own connection or change the details on an account you've already installed.

- Windows 95/98 features an Internet Setup Wizard that makes the whole process easy:

  1 Set it going by clicking the *START* button, then selecting *PROGRAMS*, then *ACCESSORIES*, then *INTERNET TOOLS*, then *INTERNET SETUP WIZARD*.

  2 Then choose the *SET UP AN INTERNET CONNECTION MANUALLY* option.

  3 Alternatively, click/double-click on the *MY COMPUTER* icon, then *DIAL-UP NETWORKING*. Click/double-click on *MAKE A NEW CONNECTION*, then follow the directions.

  4 By the end, you will have created a connection file for your ISP. When you want to connect, just click/double-click on that icon.

- The Mac Internet Setup Assistant will also take you through the process of making a new connection or re-configuring an existing one:

  1 Find the *INTERNET SETUP ASSISTANT* in the Assistants folder.

  2 Alternatively, select the *APPLE* menu, then *INTERNET ACCESS*, then *INTERNET SETUP ASSISTANT*.

In both cases, you will need to enter some technical information, addresses and telephone numbers for your ISP. They should send you what you need. Alternatively, look for Readme text file on the disc they send. The information you need should include the following:

DOMAIN NAME This is your ISP's domain name – something like **yourserviceprovider.net**.

DOMAIN NAME SERVER/IP ADDRESS Four numbers separated by full stops. This is the computer version of the domain name.

DIAL-UP TELEPHONE NUMBER The number you use to connect to your ISP.

USERNAME AND PASSWORD The name and password you chose or were assigned when you subscribed.

EMAIL ADDRESS Your own personal email address – as in **yourname@yourserviceprovider.net**.

EMAIL ACCOUNT USERNAME AND PASSWORD Relevant if you have a POP3 mail account – and you probably will.

MAIL SERVER This is the address of the computer that handles mail at your ISP – something like **mail.yourserviceprovider.net**.

NEWS SERVER The address of the computer at your ISP that handles Usenet newsgroups – usually something like **news.yourserviceprovider.net**.

This shouldn't be too confusing, but if you do have problems or if the information your ISP sent you is unclear, then contact them. It's in their interest to get you online as quickly as possible.

TROUBLESHOOTING

Despite everyone's best intentions, things don't always go smoothly. Here are a few problems you might encounter.

• **An error message flashes up saying that your modem or your dial tone wasn't detected** Your modem hasn't been installed properly. Go back and check the settings. Alternatively, you haven't plugged your modem jack into the telephone point. If you have and you still get a 'no dial tone' message, go back and check your modem settings.

- **The dial-up number your ISP gave you is engaged** More likely to happen if you're calling during peak time – in the early evening, between 7 and 10 p.m. If they encounter a busy line, many connection packages will automatically try again a few times. If this doesn't work, wait a while and then have another go. If you find it happening a lot, call your ISP to ask what's going on. If you get no answer at all, and the modem rings and rings, you may have entered the wrong telephone number. Go back and check your dial-up settings.

- **You connect but it all seems incredibly slow** Now you know why people joke about the World Wide Wait. Try connecting at different times of the day, though if you've signed up to an off-peak unmetered access deal, you may not want to do that. Sometimes things get slow because an ISP has too many subscribers online and hasn't upgraded bandwidth to cope. An efficient ISP should be able to keep things running smoothly as they grow. If things seem persistently slow, contact them and ask if they've been experiencing problems.

- **You seem to connect OK but are then refused entry** This is probably caused by problems with your password/screen name. Did you enter them correctly? Did you change them? Log off and check. Then try again.

- **The modem makes all the right noises and you seem to connect, but when you try to start up your web browser, you can't get anywhere** You probably haven't actually established a proper IP connection. Your software will usually tell you if that is the case. It could be that your software isn't configured properly. Alternatively, your ISP might be having trouble. Either way, look at your TCP/IP software and check the various addresses and names against the information sent by your ISP. Try connecting again. If you still have problems, contact your ISP.

Get your online bearings

Before you get started, it's worth taking a minute to get your bearings. To navigate successfully online, it helps to have some sort of mental picture of the net. One way of thinking of the internet is as a network of networks. This gets across the fact that the net isn't a single, coherent, unified entity, it's a multiplicity. It's always good to remember this when people try to boil the net down to one thing, and tell you that, for example, it's naturally libertarian. At a very basic level, a computer network is a collection of computers – say in an office – connected in such a way that they can communicate with each other and share information. The net takes this to a global scale. It's a global network that has emerged as more and more local and national networks hook up with each other.

To connect to and communicate with each other, computers rely on shared standard languages, or, to use the technical term, protocols. Online you'll encounter different sorts of protocol:

- When you upload or download files from the net you use FTP – File Transfer Protocol.

- The World Wide Web, the multimedia part of the net, relies on something called HTTP – Hyper Text Transfer Protocol.

- Mobile phones that let you access data services via the net use WAP – Wireless Application Protocol.

- The basic protocol which enables the net to work by letting computers round the world communicate with each other is TCP/IP – Transmission Control Protocol/Internet Protocol.

All these letters may look like the leftovers from a game of Scrabble, but after a while you will get used to them and will use them without thinking.

Another way to think about the net is as a many-to-many network. Translation? Online everyone can send as well as receive messages. In contrast, broadcast TV is a one-to-many network – one node or station sends messages and all the rest of us can do is consume those messages. Some businesses are attempting to bring the top-down, one-to-many model of TV to the net (the theory being that this will bring ordinary users online). But never forget – the net lets you send your own messages and publish your own ideas.

 Net maps You and your kids might enjoy some of the recent attempts to create different kinds of visual maps for the net. You'll find a selection at **http://www.cybergeography.org/**.

Net addresses

The net, like the real world, has a system of addresses. All computers connected to the net have a unique IP (as in Internet Protocol) address. This is a collection of four sets of numbers, separated by full stops/periods (e.g. 123.45.56.891). Incidentally, there are plans to extend and expand this system, in order to cope with the increased demand for net addresses. Obviously large groups of numbers are not the easiest things to remember (or type). So, as well as the IP addresses there is also something called the Domain Name System which translates all those numbers into words. Along with an IP address, each computer connected to the net has its own unique domain name. A few years ago, many people found these online addresses as forbidding as IP numbers. But now newspapers can now run features about the latest dot.com kids without worrying that their readers won't get the point. If you still find them a bit confusing, don't worry. They're pretty easy to figure out.

Take the address for the *Guardian*'s web site – **http://www.guardian.co.uk** .

- The first part – **http://** – refers to the protocol used to access this address, in this case Hyper Text Transfer Protocol.

- The second part – **www** – indicates which part of the net we're talking about – in this case, the World Wide Web.

- The third part – **.guardian** – is the name of the institution or people running the site/the computer it's stored on.

- The fourth part of the address – **.co** – is known as a 'top level domain'. It tells you what sort of institution is behind the site. So **.co** indicates that it's a commercial/business site.

Various other identifiers could appear here:

.ac indicates a college, university or other sort of academic establishment

.edu also indicates academic establishments, used mainly in the States

.gov a government-run site

.mil a site run by the military

.org used by non-profit organisations

.com the non-country specific version of .co, this is used by companies that want to look like global businesses

.net used mainly by internet service providers.

There are plans to add a variety of new top-level domains in the near future.

- The fifth part of the address – **.uk** – tells you in which country the site is located. These are generally pretty easy to figure out – **.jp** is Japan, **.de** is Germany, as in Deutschland, and so on. Sites that use the **.com** can get away without indicating which country they're in. To put it another way, they can present themselves as global businesses, one reason why **.com** addresses are preferred by online entrepreneurs.

The addresses for electronic mail work in the same way, with the name/nickname of the person (or department) you want to contact appearing before the basic domain name, as in **jim.mcclellan@guardian.co.uk**.

Domain names and the things people do with them are a source of endless fascination/irritation, for some net users. Early on, some people took advantage of the mainstream business world's failure to understand the net and, in a practice known as cybersquatting, bought up famous domain names, e.g. **www.bootsthechemist.co.uk**. Their hope was that the company in question would cough up serious money to get its name back. Some did, apparently. But these days the people who try that kind of thing usually end up in court. Aside from cybersquatting, a few years ago, lots of net users began to speculate in domain names, buying up words they thought might be valuable. Some did make some money selling desirable domains on to dot.com business types, though whether people are still prepared to pay up for things like **bristolhotels.co.uk** is unclear. A keen interest in domain names is a sure sign that you've become a net native.

Cybersquatting A good place to keep up with recent developments in cybersquatting is the spiky computer news site The Register **http://www.theregister.co.uk**. Just enter 'cybersquatting' in the front-page search box to catch up with the latest news.

2

Getting to grips with the net

Before you start, a quick word about the way this section is organized. I've started with the basics of the web, because that's the most popular part of the net. Email comes a close second, so you could start there instead. The section on the web also includes information about downloading files and accessing multimedia (watching video and listening to music online). The email section is followed by advice on net discussion groups and online chat. So there are two distinct strands here – one about getting information from the net and one about using the net to communicate with people. It might make sense to pick one and follow it all the way through to the end. Then again, the distinction isn't that clear-cut. So you can read these sections in whatever order you like.

The World Wide Web

The web is just one part of the net. Many people seem to think it is the net, end of story. It's true that the services you find else-where online – chatrooms, newsgroups, mailing lists – are now available on the web (albeit in a slightly different form). But strictly speaking, the web is just one part of the net, the bit where you can not only read text, but look at pictures, watch video, listen to music and more. It's also the bit that comes with an easy-to-use graphical user interface (GUI). Instead of typing complicated commands, you use the mouse to just point and click to wherever you want to go.

Tim Berners-Lee The inventor of the web, Tim Berners-Lee, is now the director of the World Wide Web Consortium. On his homepage **http://www.w3.org/People/Berners-Lee/**, you'll find talks and interviews he has given, along with information about his book, *Weaving the Web*.

The web started as an extension of an old idea – hypertext. In a hypertext document, certain words or phrases are marked as links. Click on these and you go to another document with a connection to the first – an essay on a related subject or a table of statistics. While working at CERN (the European Particle Physics Laboratory in Geneva), the British physicist Tim Berners-Lee adapted this for computer networks, so that a document stored on one computer (or server) could be linked via a network to another on a different computer.

The web may have begun life in the world of academic research. But it's now the most commercialized part of the net. However, it isn't just a global shopping mall. It isn't just about big corporate sites and net shops. It still has a human dimension. It still lets ordinary individuals tell the world exactly what they're thinking, via their own personal websites.

How the web can benefit your family:

- It's simple really. The web offers easy access to all sorts of information. Your kids can research their schoolwork on the web. They can learn more about their hobbies and leisure pursuits. They can find out more about their favourite stars, films and TV shows. You can access information that can help with parenting – everything from advice on places to go to medical problems and school reports.

- The web is a multimedia experience, enabling your kids to watch video clips, listen to music and play games. There's more on this on page 96.

- There are lots of special kids' sites on the web that host supervised chatrooms and discussion groups where they can swap ideas with other children.

- Via the web, they can download free software, interactive toys and more – there's more on this on page 82.

- You and your kids can put up your own webpages – things devoted to family history or their favourite toys/books/music. Children can also see pages created by other kids from around the world. Your kids will get a real sense of achievement from this, and their efforts might even compare favourably with the work done by big companies. There's more information about this on page 178.

- You can shop via the web – very useful for parents who don't always have the time to get out. You can save money as well as time, if you shop carefully. You can find those hard to get toys and do the supermarket shopping without leaving home. More on this on page 165.

Potential problems with the web that parents need to be aware of:

- The web is filled with adult information and content (which doesn't just mean porn), and it's potentially as easy for your children to access this as it is for them to visit a website devoted to Digimon or Hear'say.

- A homepage on the web is publicly accessible. It can be seen by anyone. So you need to make sure your children don't reveal any personal information that might be used by others who don't have their best interests at heart.

- Lots of sites offer free gifts to kids in return for information about themselves and sometimes their parents. You need to teach kids not to give out personal data to any site that asks, but to ask you first.

- If you leave your credit card information lying around – for example, in a file on your computer – your kids will be able to go on a spending spree online and you might end up picking up the tab.

- Putting up a flashy-looking web site is relatively cheap and easy. Adults have been conned by sites that look the part but are in fact fly-by-night scams. You need to teach your kids how to check out a site.

- There's lots of dubious information on the web that might look 'official' and 'credible' but is in fact a load of hokum. You need to teach your kids to be sceptical about what they read on the web.

There are things you can do to counter all these potential problems. Some involve buying special bits of software, but most come down to talking to your kids and thinking ahead about what they might get up to online. There's more information on page 244.

Webpages, websites and homepages Let's get these straight before we go any further. A webpage is a document, usually formatted in HTML. A website is a collection of pages put up by an individual, institution or business. A homepage can be: (a) the first page your browser shows when it starts; or (b) the first page of a website. But most non-geeky types now think of a homepage as a personal website put up by an ordinary net user.

Software

To access the web, you need a web browser. There are two big players in the browser business – Microsoft and Netscape – and your computer, if bought new, is likely to come bundled with one or the other.

- Netscape's browser used to be called Navigator. It was then subsumed into Communicator, a 'suite' of net tools. The latest version of that suite of tools is now just called Netscape 6. Navigator is still part of it, but to avoid confusion, I'll just refer to it throughout as Netscape 6.

- Microsoft's browser is Internet Explorer. You can get this in the basic browser version or with all sorts of extra programs.

Which browser should you use? To be honest, there's not much to choose between the big two.

- Both are multimedia devices capable of handling sound, video and 3D graphics.

- Both are multi-purpose net tools you can use to do your email, download software from FTP sites, read newsgroups and more.

- Those who despise Bill Gates and all his works may want to go with Netscape. Then again, Netscape is owned by AOL, so it isn't exactly an anti-corporate option.

In terms of reliability and performance, Internet Explorer probably has the edge – and it is the more popular of the two. That said, Netscape 6 is improving all the time.

In the end, the choice is yours.

Older computers and browsers If you are trying to get online using an old computer with limited disk space and RAM, especially if you're running an old operating system like Windows 3.x, you'll need to use an older browser. Try Internet Explorer 3.x or Netscape 2.x. Alternatively, try to get hold of Opera **http://www.opera.com**, a quick and compact 'indie' browser that compares well with the big two.

In the following pages, you'll find detailed advice on using Internet Explorer 5.5 and Netscape 6.1, since these were the most current versions as we went to press (an early public preview of Internet Explorer 6 had just become available). Your ISP should supply you with a version of either, though some just send you Internet Explorer. If you really don't like the browser they send you, go online to **http://www.microsoft.com** or **http://www.netscape.com** and get the other one. (There's advice on how to do this on page 82.) In general, the Mac versions of the browsers are roughly the same as their Windows counterparts. Netscape generally does a better job than Microsoft when it comes to making its Mac and Windows browsers roughly the same. When there are differences that might be confusing, I'll point them out as we go along. Both browsers have menu links that take you directly to webpages where you can get new versions/upgrades. It's useful to check in to these every now and then, especially if you use Internet Explorer – there are always lots of bug fixes and security updates on the Microsoft page.

- In Internet Explorer:
  1 Get online and select the *TOOLS* menu, then *WINDOWS UPDATE*.
  2 You'll go to a page where you can download Windows-related upgrades and extras.

- In Netscape 6:
  1 Get online and click the toolbar link to **netscape.co.uk**, then click the *DOWNLOAD* button at the top of the page.
  2 You'll go to a page where you can download various upgrades.

AOL and the web If you get online with AOL, you need to have Internet Explorer 5.x as your browser. Once you do connect, you'll discover that AOL puts its own interface on top of IE5. You get a whole series of toolbar buttons that take you quickly to AOL content, which is fine, but you get less functionality when it comes to browsing the web, which isn't. One way round this is to use AOL to establish a connection, minimize the AOL window, then start your IE5 or Netscape 6 and use that instead.

Surfing the web for the first time

Get online, then start your browser (click/double-click on its icon on your desktop). When it loads, you'll most likely see either a Microsoft start page (if you're using Explorer) or the Netscape homepage (if you're using Navigator). Alternatively, your ISP may have configured your browser so that you go to their site. (You can change your browser homepage – more on this later.) On the page that loads, you should see:

- Text, graphics, pictures and little icons.

- A scroll bar on the right that lets you move up and down the page.

- Highlighted or underlined words: these are hypertext links. Move your cursor over the highlighted words – the arrow changes to a pointing finger, indicating a clickable link. Click on this and you move to another webpage – either on the same computer or on another one on the other side of the world.

- Colourful banner ads, usually featuring eye-catching animations – if you're on a corporate page. Click on these and you'll go to the site they're advertising.

Pop-up ads In the last few years, online ads have become more invasive. They now split up articles, move across pages and appear in separate windows that pop up over the thing you actually want to access. A few years ago, only porn sites used pop-up ads. Now all sorts of reputable sites have them. You don't have to wait for them to load. If one pops up, just close it straight away. Incidentally, if you're on a site that opens loads of pop-up windows when you arrive and when you leave, it's a good sign that it's a dodgy operation.

You may also encounter frames, image maps and forms.

- Frames are different sections within a browser window. You might have a basic document in the main part of the window, with an index to the website as a whole framed off on the left. Clicking on a link in the index in the left frame will cause a new page to open in the large main frame.

- Image maps are large graphic images, different portions of which are links to other documents. As you move the cursor over the image, you'll see the pointing finger appear, indicating the links.

- Forms are like forms in real life. Just click in the dialog box, type in the information, then look for a *SEND* button to click. You can refine the information you send via drop-down menus. Just click on the arrow pointing down to bring up a menu, select the relevant category, click, then move on to the next question.

OK – let's surf.

1 Move the cursor over a link and click on it. If you haven't picked an email link, another page will load.

2 Find a link on that and click on it. You'll go to another page.

3 Find a link and click that, and another page will come up.

Congratulations. You're surfing. Not that hard really, and, as you can now see, the term is a little grandiose for such a sedentary activity. The conventional wisdom is that people surfed a lot in the past, but now they just go direct to the sites they want. I'm not sure if that's true. Sometimes it's still interesting to just ramble around and see what turns up.

Surfing One those bits of net slang everyone loves to hate. If you can't stand the term, blame Jean Armour Polly, who is officially accepted as the person who first came up with it back in 1992. Find out more at **http://www.netmom.com/about/surfingmezz.shtml**. Incidentally, the Net Mom site is a very useful resource for parents and kids.

The buttons on the main toolbar are the easiest to use for basic navigation:

1 If a page starts to appear that you don't like, click the *STOP* button. That stops the page from loading.

2 Click the *BACK* button and you'll return to your previous page. Click the *FORWARD* button and – surprise, surprise – you'll go forward to the page you just left.

3 If you've followed a long set of links and just want to get back to your home/start page, click the *HOME* button.

4 As you go back through pages you've visited, you'll see that the links you clicked have changed colour. It's a simple way of helping you keep track.

How about going to a site you select for yourself? Let's try the *Guardian*'s site. For this, you'll need the *Guardian*'s URL (it stands for Uniform Resource Locator) or web address – **http://www.guardian.co.uk**. Web addresses are the sum of a few standard parts.

• The protocol **http** stands for HyperText Transfer Protocol and is used to send webpages across a network.

• The domain name of the computer that hosts the site **www.guardian.co.uk**. In this case, the computer is a web server – hence the **www** bit.

• The *Guardian* URL ends there, but URLs can specify a specific document (e.g. **document.html**) and the directories in which it's stored.

The problem with guessing URLs You want to find the site put by your child's favourite celebrity. You don't know what the URL is, but you figure it could be their name, plus .com or .co.uk. You're probably right. However, in the past, dodgy types have registered the dot.com addresses of famous names and put up porn sites there. Madonna, Zoë Ball and Mel B from the Spice Girls have all suffered from this. So if you're guessing, you might want to check this while your kids are otherwise occupied, just so they don't get any nasty surprises.

Click in the location bar at the top of your browser, just underneath the main tool bar, then delete the address that's there. Type in the *Guardian* URL, then hit *ENTER/RETURN* or click on the little *GO* button at the right end of the location bar. Alternatively:

- **In Internet Explorer:**
  1 Select the *FILE* menu, then *OPEN*.
  2 Write the URL in the text box and click *OK*.

- **In Netscape 6:**
  1 Select the *FILE* menu, then *OPEN WEB LOCATION*.
  2 Write the URL in the text box.
  3 Via the drop-down menu below the text box, you can choose to open the page you want in the current window, or a new one. Then click *OPEN*.

- **In Internet Explorer for the Mac:**
  1 Select the *FILE* menu, then *OPEN LOCATION*.
  2 Write the URL in the text box and click *OK*.
  3 Alternatively, just write the URL in the location bar and click the *GO* button.

Entering URLs correctly Throughout the book, I've written all the web addresses out in full, with the **http://** bit at the beginning. You don't need to enter this when you write a URL in the location bar – your browser will add it for you. Incidentally, not every URL comes with a **www** prefix: some just start with the name of the server: **guardian.co.uk** or whatever. Finally, however they may appear in this book, web addresses do not end in full stops . So, to recap, ignore the **http://** and any full stops at the end. Otherwise, enter them exactly as given.

Mouse menus

Using the left mouse button to click on a link will bring up that link (or download a file or an image). Right-click on something on a webpage – a link, an image, even the page background – and a 'mouse menu' will appear, offering you various options (saving the page, or opening a link or some such). Here's a simple navigational trick that mouse menus make easy. At some point on the web you will find yourself waiting for a page to load. You can open up a new browser window and check out another webpage while you wait. Using two or more browser windows at once can be useful if you're looking at a page of useful links. You can keep that page open and explore the links in new windows.

- In Internet Explorer:
  1 Right-click on the link you're interested in, then select *OPEN IN A NEW WINDOW*.
  2 Alternatively, select the *FILE* menu, then *NEW*, then *WINDOW*, then

enter the address of the new page you want to look at in the location bar.

- **In Netscape 6:**

  1 Right-click on the link you're interested in, then select *OPEN IN A NEW WINDOW*.

  2 Alternatively, select the *FILE* menu, then *OPEN WEB LOCATION*, write the URL you want in the text box, then, via the drop-down menu below the text box, choose to open the page you want in a new window. Then click *OPEN*.

- **Mac users don't have a second mouse button, so they can't right-click. However, with newer Macs (and the newer browsers), you can call up mouse menus with a sort of delayed action click:**

  1 Click on a link, but hold down the mouse button. Don't let it click.

  2 A mouse menu should appear. Choose the option you want all the while holding down the button.

  3 Then release the button, letting it click.

More complex navigation

The *BACK/FORWARD* buttons are useful enough, but if you build up a longer trail, then want to get back to an early page, you'll need something else.

- In Internet Explorer, look at the *BACK/FORWARD* toolbar buttons. There's a little inverted triangle to the side of each. Move your cursor over it and it turns into a button. Click on it and a list of sites appears. Click on the one you want.

- In Netscape 6, you can pull the same trick with the *BACK/FORWARD* buttons. Alternatively, select the *GO* menu and at the bottom, you'll see a list of sites previously visited. Select the one you want.

With both browsers, you can also pull down a list of the URLs you entered in the location bar by clicking on the pull-down menu at the right side of the box.

The above methods don't always work. Say you're on a site and you follow a set of links through it to a page you want, then use the *BACK* button to come back to the front page, then follow a new set of links to a different document on the same site. The new trail of links will be recorded over the previous set, so that when you use the *GO* menu or the *BACK/FORWARD* menus, you'll only see that latest trail. For a proper list of all the pages you've visited, you need to access History, a list of sites you've visited in this particular session (and over previous days). To access this:

- **In Internet Explorer:**
  1 Click the *HISTORY* button on the toolbar (or the *HISTORY* tab if you're using the Mac version).
  2 The history list will open in a separate frame on the left of your main browser window.
  3 Click on the site you want and it will come up in the main window.
  4 To remove the separate frame, click the *HISTORY* button again.

- **In Netscape 6:**
  1 Select the *TASKS* menu, then *TOOLS*, then *HISTORY*.
  2 A separate window will open showing the sites you visited.
  3 Click on the one you want and it will open in the main window.

You can use History while you're online. But you can also go offline and use it to view sites you've previously visited – this is known as offline browsing. If you're using a free ISP and paying your phone bills, this may save you some money.

- **In Internet Explorer:**
  1 Select the *FILE* menu, then *WORK OFFLINE*.
  2 Then click the *HISTORY* button.

- **In Netscape 6:**
  1 Select the *FILE* menu, then *WORK OFFLINE*.
  2 Then access *HISTORY* as normal.

You can specify how long you want your browser to keep details of pages in History.

- **In Internet Explorer:**
  1 Select the *TOOLS* menu, then *INTERNET OPTIONS*.
  2 Look for a section on History on the General dialog box, where you'll be able to change the number in the box next to the line 'Days to keep pages in history', then click *OK*.

- **In Netscape 6:**
  1 Select the *EDIT* menu, then *PREFERENCES*.
  2 Click on *NAVIGATOR* to reveal the Navigator menu, then click on *HISTORY*. In the resulting dialog box, change the number in the box next to 'Pages in history expire after X days', then click *OK*.

- **In the Mac version of Internet Explorer:**
  1 Select the *EDIT* menu, then *PREFERENCES*.
  2 An Internet Explorer *PREFERENCES* dialog box will appear.
  3 In the category box on the left, select *ADVANCED* in the Web Browser section. Then change the figure in the History section as required.

History is an interface for documents stored in a file called the cache. If you extend your history file, but don't also allow more disk space for your browser's cache, you won't be able to access some of the earlier entries (there's more on the cache below). If you feel weighed down by the past, in both browsers there's a *CLEAR HISTORY* button in the section where you specify the size of the history file.

> **History and kids** Via History, you can keep a discreet eye on what your kids have been looking at on the web. Of course, it will also let them to see what you've been browsing, so if you look at sites you don't want them to see, clear History once you're done. If History is clear after your kids have been browsing online for a while, it may be a sign that they're trying to hide something from you. You can find out what they were looking at by looking in the cache – more on this shortly. If the cache is empty too, you'll know that your kids know their way round the PC and that they're definitely trying to hide something from you.

Getting to your favourite sites faster

Browsers let you keep a list of your favourite sites, so you can access them a bit quicker.

- **In Internet Explorer:**
  1 If you're on the page you want to mark, select the *FAVOURITES* menu, then *ADD TO FAVOURITES*.
  2 Alternatively, just right-click in an empty part of the page, then select *ADD TO FAVOURITES* from the mouse menu.
  3 An Add Favourite dialog box will come up. Ignore all the stuff about subscribing to the site and tick the option to add the page to your Favourites list, then *OK*.

To use your IE Favourites list:

1 Click the *FAVOURITES* button on the toolbar. It will open in a frame on the left.

2 Click the site you want and (if you're online) it will load in the right-hand window.

3 To remove the frame, click the *FAVOURITES* button again.

4 Alternatively, you can use the Favourites menu to view your list.

- **In Netscape 6:**

   1 Click the *BOOKMARK* button (which is under the location bar), then select *ADD BOOKMARK*.

   2 Alternatively, right-click on an empty space on the page and select *ADD BOOKMARK* from the mouse menu.

To access your bookmarks:

1 Click the *BOOKMARK* button and a list will come up.

2 Click on the site you want to go to.

It's pretty easy to build up a big file of Bookmarks/Favourites after a while. So start filing them in specific folders as soon as possible.

- **In Internet Explorer:**

   1 Select the *FAVOURITES* menu, then *ORGANIZE FAVOURITES*.

- **In Netscape:**

   1 Click the *BOOKMARKS* button then select *FILE BOOKMARK*.

Kids and bookmarks

Some sites have attempted to benefit from the typos you and your kids might make when entering URLs. They use addresses that are slight mis-spellings of popular sites like Yahoo! and Netscape. Some of these sites are advertising scams – the idea is to lure people to sites and rack up page impressions, so that the site owners can charge more for ads on the site. Some of these sites feature porn. Another thing to look out for: some dubious operators have put up porn sites whose addresses are deliberately close to those of popular mainstream sites. For example, **www.whitehouse.gov** is the online home of the American President, but **www.whitehouse.com** is a porn site. NASA has also had problems with sites that use its name and a different top level domain (as in **.org**, **.com** or **.net**). Book-marking the sites your children use a lot is one way of avoiding this kind of thing.

Watch your own bookmarks If you use the same browser as your children, you may end up bookmarking sites you don't want them to see. But they'll be there in the Bookmarks/Favourites file, just a click away. One thing you can do is to pick a very boring name for them when you set the Bookmark/Favourite up – something to do with your work, for example. Then they won't be tempted.

TROUBLESHOOTING

Sometimes you won't be able to get to a particular site. Your browser will usually tell you what the problem is and flash up some sort of error message. Here are a few problems you may encounter.

- **Your browser says it is unable to locate the server or that the server doesn't have a DNS entry.** Check that you entered the URL correctly. If you did, try again. If you get the same error message, the server at the site may be down or the site may have closed down.

- **A message comes up saying that the 'Connection was refused by Host'.** The site you're trying to access is probably very busy. Try again, and if you get the same message, leave it until a different time of the day.

- **You seem to get through to the site, but a page comes up saying File Not Found.** The page you're looking for may have been moved during a re-design. You can usually find the document you want by working back through the site URL. For example, if **http://www.hipsite.com/index/television/simpsons.html** doesn't work, it may be that the document **simpsons.html** is now in a different directory. Click in the location bar, delete **/index/television/simpsons.html**, leave **http://www.hipsite.com** intact and hit the *ENTER/ RETURN* key. You'll go to the front page of **hipsite.com**. From there, look for links to the document you want.

- **You get an error message saying that the Document contains no data.** Most URLs end with a web document – in the example above, the document is **simpsons.html**. With URLs that don't end with **.html** or **.htm**, the browser will look for a default document – something like **index.html**. If there isn't one, it can get confused and show the above error message. Access the site's front page (by taking the directory path out of the URL, as above) and look for a link to the page you want.

- **You get into the site you want, but things move very slowly and the page seems to seize up.** Another problem caused by excess traffic on a site. Sometimes all you can do is wait, and keep track of progress via the *STATUS* bar in the bottom left of the browser, which tells you roughly how much of the page has loaded. Sometimes you can get somewhere by hitting the *STOP* button, then the *RELOAD* button (in Netscape 6) or the *REFRESH* button (in Internet Explorer). Your browser will try to get the page again and this time you might be able to get through.

- **You're on a page, you click a link and nothing happens or the wrong page comes up.** Broken links are less common nowadays, but they're still around. The average website usually offers several different routes to its various sections. So look around on the front page for an alternative link to the page you want.

Customizing your browser

Your browser is set to do certain things by default – for example, load your ISP's site as the homepage. You can personalize your browser and speed up your web surfing by making a few changes. First, try altering your browser's homepage.

- **In Internet Explorer:**
  1 Select the *TOOLS* menu, then *INTERNET OPTIONS*.
  2 In the *GENERAL* dialog box, in the *HOME PAGE* section, enter the URL you (or your kids) want in the *ADDRESS* box.
  3 The *USE BLANK* button means your browser will show a blank page as its homepage, which will make it load quicker.

- **In Netscape 6:**
  1 Select the *EDIT* menu, then *PREFERENCES*.
  2 In the *NAVIGATOR* dialog box, you can choose a blank page, or, in the *HOME PAGE* section, enter your chosen URL in the *LOCATION* box.
  3 You can also use your bookmarks as a homepage. They're stored in a page called **bookmark.htm**.

You can also remove some of the toolbars so that you can see more of the webpage you're accessing. To try out the various toolbar options in Internet Explorer and Netscape 6, select the *VIEW* menu. Try out various permutations to see what you're comfortable with (i.e. which buttons and menus you actually need when you're wandering round the web).

....

Customizing Netscape 6's My Sidebar

....

The little frames to the left of the main window that display *HISTORY* and *FAVOURITES* in Internet Explorer 5 are called 'browser bars'. Netscape 6 has a similar feature, called *MY SIDEBAR*. You can get it to appear by selecting the *VIEW* menu then *MY SIDEBAR*. Basically, it's a way of displaying certain useful links in a separate frame to the side of the main browser window. Lots of these links are loaded by default and are themed around different areas – weather, technology, news, travel etc. These can be useful. You can also get *MY SIDEBAR* to display your *BOOKMARKS* and *HISTORY* the way IE5 does via its browser bars. Display *MY SIDEBAR* then click the *TABS* button at the top right then click *CUSTOMIZE SIDEBAR*. Click *RECOMMENDED* in the left window. Click on either *HISTORY* or *BOOKMARKS* (or both), then *ADD,* then *OK*. Once they're there, you just click the relevant tab and *HISTORY* or *BOOKMARKS* will come up in *MY SIDEBAR*.

The cache and saving documents and images from the web

Every page you visit is saved by your browser in a file known as a cache (Internet Explorer calls the cache its 'Temporary Internet Files'.) The idea is to speed up your browsing and do a little towards saving the net's limited resources. Whenever you visit a site, your browser will first check in its cache to see if it already has the relevant page. And when you click the *BACK/FORWARD* button, rather than getting the page all over again, your browser retrieves it from the cache. You can improve your browsing speed by changing some of the cache settings.

- In Internet Explorer:

  1 Select the *TOOLS* menu, then *INTERNET OPTIONS*, then the *GENERAL* tab.

  2 In the *TEMPORARY INTERNET FILES* section, click the *SETTINGS* button.

  3 You can then specify how much disk space you want the cache to use. The bigger you make the cache, the more it can store to call on during revisits. However, you don't want to overload your hard disk, so don't go mad – more than half the total size of your hard disk is probably a bit much.

  4 In the *CHECK FOR NEWER VERSIONS OF STORED PAGES* section, make sure that *EVERY TIME YOU START INTERNET EXPLORER* is selected. This means your browser will check the page if you haven't yet visited it in the current session online, but if you have, it will get the stored version from the cache.

  5 If your cache gets too full, it can slow down your browsing. To clear it and free up disk space, click the *EMPTY FOLDER* button in the *TEMPORARY INTERNET FILES* section.

6 If you want to see what's in the cache, in the *TEMPORARY INTERNET FILES* section, click the *SETTINGS* button, then the *VIEW FILES* button.

- **In Netscape 6:**

  1 Select the *EDIT* menu, then *PREFERENCES*, then *CACHE* (it's in the *ADVANCED* section) to call up the relevant dialog box.

  2 With Netscape 6 you have to enter the amount of space for both the Memory Cache and Disk Cache – so you need to know how much space you have to play around with. It's probably not a good idea to go for less than the default.

  3 With the line 'Compare the page in the cache to page on the network', it's probably best to tick 'Once per session'.

  4 To clear the cache and free up disk space, click both the *CLEAR MEMORY CACHE* and *CLEAR DISK CACHE* buttons in the Cache dialog box.

- **In the Mac version of Internet Explorer:**

  1 Select the *EDIT* menu, then *PREFERENCES*.

  2 Then click on *ADVANCED* in the Web Browser section.

  3 To clear the cache and free up disk space, click the *EMPTY NOW* button.

Saving and printing web pages

If you find a page you know you'll want to refer back to, you can always save it to your hard disk. If you're saving a page with frames, click in the frame you're interested in before you start. If all you want is the image from a particular page, right-click on the image, then choose *SAVE IMAGE AS* (in Netscape 6) or *SAVE PICTURE AS* (in Internet Explorer) from the mouse menu. To save a whole page:

- **In Internet Explorer:**

  1 Select the *FILE* menu, then *SAVE AS*.

  2 You can choose to save the page as a complete webpage (or 'web archive'). If you choose the former, when you open it again (with an application that can handle HTML, like your browser), it will retain the basic formatting it had on the web.

  3 If you choose *TEXT*, all you get is the text and some basic formatting.

- **In Netscape 6:**

  1 Select the *FILE* menu, then *SAVE AS*.

  2 Netscape 6 lets you save all the files connected with a page. If you just want to save it as an html document, select the *FILE* menu, then *EDIT*. Then select the *FILE* menu in the new window that appears, then *SAVE AS*.

Rather than save webpages that seem particularly useful, you can print them out for future reference. (Incidentally, if you want to print an individual frame, right-click in the frame, then select *PRINT* from the mouse menu.)

- **In Internet Explorer:**

  1 Select the *FILE* menu, then *PRINT*.

  2 In the *PRINT* dialog box, make sure *ALL* is ticked in the *PRINT RANGE* section.

  3 If you want to see whether the page is going to look something like it does on screen, or if you want to pick out certain pages to print, select the *FILE* menu, then *PRINT PREVIEW*. Select the *FILE* menu, then *PRINT*, then specify the pages you want.

- **In Netscape 6:**

  1 The easiest thing to do is use the *PRINT* button on the toolbar – it's on the right of the location bar.

  2 In the dialog box that appears, you can choose to print the whole document or selected pages.

Browsing tips The specialist net magazines are a good source for browser tips and tricks. *.net* does a page about Internet Explorer 5 **http://www.netmag.co.uk/ie5/default.htm**, where you can find out more about IE5's hidden depths. For more information about Netscape 6, try **http://home.netscape.com/browsers/6/index.html** or the Unofficial Netscape 6 FAQ **http://home.adelphia.net/~sremick/ns6faq.html**. If you're using an older Netscape browser, you can find some useful tips at **http://home.netscape.com/browsers/using/** or the Unofficial Netscape FAQ **http://www.ufaq.org**. FAQ, by the way, stands for 'Frequently Asked Questions' – an FAQ is the net equivalent of a basic guidebook/user's manual.

Searching the web

So now you know how to move around the web. The next step is learning how to find the information you want. There are a couple of online resources that can help you here:

- **Search engines** These rely on autonomous software programs ('bots') that roam the web collecting details about different pages (the URL, the title, the keywords or 'meta tags' chosen by the creator of the page as a summary of its content, and usually the whole text of a page). A database is created from the bot's findings. Users then search this and turn up links to different sites, grouped in order of relevance.

- **Directories** These offer collections of links, arranged into different categories and themes. The directories employ people to assemble their lists of sites. But some also use bots. They also accept submissions sent in by site webmasters. You can use a search engine to search a directory's links. But you can also drill down through different directories looking for the sites you want.

Actually, the distinction between search engines and directories is so blurred nowadays as to be pretty useless. It's better to refer to them all as search sites.

How search sites can benefit your family:

- Pretty obvious really. Often you know the site you want to access. But if you don't, if you just have a subject you want to research, search engines will show you the wealth of information online relating to your particular interest.

Potential problems with search sites that parents need to be aware of:

- Search engines are only machines. If you use vague search terms that could be read in different ways – for example, 'girls' toys' –

you may turn up links to sites that aren't suitable for kids

- Information overload – again, if you don't refine your search terms, you can get snowed under by non-relevant search results.

The search sites are some of the busiest and best-known online locations. Even if you've never been on the net, you'll probably have heard of Yahoo!. The leading search sites are:

About.com http://www.about.com

AltaVista http://www.altavista.com

Excite http://www.excite.com
http://www.excite.co.uk

FAST Search http://www.alltheweb.com

Google http://www.google.com

Hotbot http://hotbot.lycos.com/

Look Smart http://www.looksmart.com
http://www.looksmart.co.uk

Lycos http://www.lycos.com
http://www.lycos.co.uk

Northern Light http://www.northernlight.com

Open Directory http://dmoz.org

Yahoo! http://www.yahoo.com
http://www.yahoo.co.uk

Most of the sites mentioned are fine, though my favourite is Google, mainly because it seems to deliver more relevant results than the rest. It does it by ranking its search results according to how many other sites link to each entry. It also takes into account the ranking of those sites doing the linking. The idea is that if a lot of highly ranked sites link to a particular site in a particular field, it's more likely to be relevant in some way to the original query. This may sound a bit complex, but it seems to work.

Though the search engines are getting better, they still don't cover anything like the whole web. There might be great sites out there about pets or Rumble Robots that you'll never be able to find for your kids, because the search site you're using hasn't logged them yet. So what can you do?

- To search more of the web, try the 'metasearch' sites which let you use several major search engines at once. Have a look at MetaCrawler **http://www.metacrawler.com/**, Dogpile **http://www.dogpile.com**, and Search.com **http://www.search.com**.

- Alternatively, download Copernic **http://www.copernic.com**, a search agent program that lets you work with lots of search sites at once.

- To find out which search engine is currently deemed to be the best, try Search Engine Watch **http://www.searchenginewatch.com/**.

- Alternatively, visit About.com's Web Search page **http://websearch.about.com/**. This has news and reviews, plus advice on better searching.

Using a search engine

With search engines, you can just dive straight in, enter the subject you want to research in the text box and click the *SEARCH* button. You'll probably turn up something useful. But you'll also probably get lots of links with little or no connection to the subject you're interested in. Why? If you don't enter your search terms properly, most search engines do a general search on all the words in your query. They will turn up pages that feature them all, pages that feature some and pages that feature only one. As you can imagine, that's a lot of pages. To get useful results, you need to learn how to use a search engine properly. This mainly involves entering the right search terms.

Some search sites can handle natural language queries – as in "Where can I find a website about fishing?" Ask Jeeves **http://www.ask.co.uk** is the leader in this field, though standard search sites like AltaVista **http://www.altavista.com** now allow for something similar. But with most search sites you have to follow certain rules when entering search terms. Whichever search site you use, read the Help file first to find out how it works. As an example of what to do, here are the Google guidelines:

- To enter a query, just type some relevant terms into the text box and click on the Google *SEARCH* button. For example, to plan a holiday to Hawaii, you should type *holiday hawaii* in the text box. Unlike some search engines, Google only returns those pages that include all of your search terms. In addition, Google also gives a higher ranking to those pages in which your query terms appear near each other.

- To restrict a search further, just add more terms. For example, *cats pets homes* will yield more relevant results than just *cats*.

- One thing that may trip you up. Google ignores common words, which it refers to as stop words. It disregards words like 'the', 'where' and 'how', as well as some single digit numbers and single letters. They say that these terms usually don't help when searching and can slow things down. You can make sure stop words are included, by using the '+' sign. Make sure you include a space before the '+' sign. So to search for 'Star Wars, Episode 1', you'd have to enter *Star Wars Episode +1* in the text box.

- You can use the minus sign to exclude certain terms from your search. Just put '-' in front of the term you want to exclude. A search for *bass -music* will generally return pages about fish rather than musicians. Make sure you include a space before the minus sign.

- To search for specific phrases or names on Google, add quotation marks. Words enclosed in double quotation marks, as in "Martin Amis", will appear together in the results that are turned up. If the phrase includes a Google stop word, you'll need to use the '+' sign to make sure it gets included.

- Google treats hyphens, slashes, periods/full stops, equals signs, and apostrophes as 'phrase connectors'. These connect words – so if you enter mother-in-law, it's treated as a phrase even though the words aren't in quotation marks.

- To use Google to search for pages containing either word A or word B, use a capitalized 'OR' between terms. So to search for a holiday in either London or Paris, you'd have to type *holiday london OR paris*.

- As you'll see from this example, searches on Google are not case-sensitive. Everything you enter in the text box is treated as lower case.

- You can restrict a search on Google to its own directory, directory.google.com. If you search for Saturn within the Science > Astronomy section of the directory, you'll only get links to pages about the planet. You won't get links to pages about Saturn cars or the old Sega Saturn game console.

- You can further restrict some searches on Google via certain 'operators'. For example, if you want to search a specific domain or site, use the 'site' operator. So to search the *Guardian* site for information about privacy, enter *privacysite:www.guardian.co.uk* in the text box.

- Unlike lots of search sites, Google doesn't let you do 'wildcard' searches. On some other search sites, if you tack the asterisk on to the end of a word, they will search for other similarly spelled words that contain up to five additional letters. So a search using the term *breed** will look for breed, breeders and breeding. Google, by contrast, searches for the words exactly as you enter them in the search box.

- However, it does offer an alternative spellings service, in which, after you've entered a search term, you're asked whether you actually meant another word.

- Incidentally, Google allows you to refine your searches further (e.g. you can ask for results only in certain languages) via the Advanced Search link.

> **Search engines and kids** As mentioned above, vague/ambiguous search terms can generate results that aren't suitable for kids. To combat this, some search sites let you set up a family filter that cuts out all 'adult' content from the results it serves up. AltaVista, Google and Lycos all offer this service. You should find a link to a page where you can set this up on the site homepage – you'll find Google's safe search function via the Preferences link.

The other search engines work in roughly the same way, though each has it own quirks. So you really do need to read those help pages before you start.

Let's try a search on Google:

1 Use the guidelines to sort your search terms. Then enter them in the text box and click the Google *SEARCH* button.

2 After a while, Google will take you to a results screen, which will probably tell you that it has found thousands of pages that fit your search. It ranks the pages found in terms of relevance and shows you links to the top ten.

3 You should see the title of the page, plus the address, then an excerpt from the webpage, which shows how your search terms are used in context on that page.

4 The search terms should be in bold, so you can tell quickly whether the result is a page you want to visit.

5   Click one of the links on the results page and you'll go to the site in question. To get back to the results page, hit the *BACK* button.

6   At the end of the text about each site in your results list, you should also see a link to Similar Pages. Click this and you'll turn up pages related to this particular result.

Browsers and searching

Navigator and Internet Explorer both have Search toolbar buttons that provide quick links to search sites.

- **In Internet Explorer:**

  1   Click the *SEARCH* button (or the *SEARCH* tab in the Mac version) and a browser bar with a search box inside it will open.

  2   Enter your search terms in the box and click on *SEARCH*. Your search results will appear in the browser bar.

  3   Click on the links shown and the site comes up in the main window (while the search results remain in the browser bar).

  4   If you want to see the search engines you're using (and remove one or two), click the *CUSTOMIZE* button.

- **In Netscape 6:**

  1   Click the *SEARCH* button and you go to Netscape's search page, where you'll find links to all the big sites.

  2   Alternatively, if you've set up *MY SIDEBAR* with a *SEARCH* tab, click that.

  3   A search box will appear in the sidebar. You can enter your search terms and then choose to search via Netscape Search UK, Google, Lycos and more. The results appear in the main window.

  4   If you choose to search via Netscape, a selection of the best results will also appear in *MY SIDEBAR* below the search text box. Click on a link, and the page loads in the main window.

- **Mac Users**

    1   Apart from the *SEARCH* buttons, if you have a newer Mac, you can also use its built-in search tool, Sherlock.

    2   In Internet Explorer, you can start Sherlock up via the *APPLE* menu.

Both browsers now have a What's Related function, which uses technology from a program called Alexa **http://www.alexa.com** to call up lists of sites that previous users thought were similar to the site you're accessing now. It can point you in interesting directions.

- **In Internet Explorer:**

    1   Select the *TOOLS* menu, then *SHOW RELATED LINKS*.

- **In Netscape 6:**

    1   You can access *WHAT'S RELATED* via *MY SIDEBAR*.

    2   Add the feature by clicking the *TABS* button on the top right of *MY SIDEBAR*, then selecting *CUSTOMIZE SIDEBAR*. Click on *RECOMMENDED* to find *WHAT'S RELATED*, click that, then *ADD*, then *OK*.

- **In the Mac version of Internet Explorer:**

    1   You can access *WHAT'S RELATED* via the *TOOLS* menu.

Using an online directory

If messing around with + and – signs to define a search isn't your thing, you might prefer an online directory, where you can just click through various directories and sub-directories in search of the subject you want (and the links to the sites that cover it). Take the opening page of Yahoo!,

http://www.yahoo.co.uk. Here you'll see fourteen or so general headings – Arts and Humanities, Business and Economy, Education, News and Media, Reference, Society and Culture and many others. Under each general heading is a selection of sub-headings. So under Society and Culture, you see People, Environment, Royalty and Religion. Each of these headings and sub-headings is a clickable link. Click it and you move to that area of the directory, where you find more links.

As an example, let's look at Yahoo!'s list of web search tools.

1 Look for the *COMPUTERS AND INTERNET* heading. Underneath you'll see several sub-headings – Internet, WWW, Software, Multimedia. Click on *WWW*.

2 This will take you to the general World Wide Web section. At the top you'll see links which take you to UK or Ireland-only sites in the general category. Below is another set of general categories to do with the web, from ActiveX and Announcement Services to Web-based Entertainment and XML.

3 By some of these categories, you may notice the @ sign. This indicates that this section cross-references with another general category. So if you click *ACTIVEX@*, it will take you to the *COMPUTERS AND INTERNET: SOFTWARE* section.

4 Actually, the exact location of this section is shown at the top in a list of all the directories it is nested within, as in *Home > Computers_and_Internet > Software > Operating_Systems > Windows > Windows_95 > Information_and_Documentation > ActiveX*. This kind of directory chain appears at the top of every page in Yahoo!. If you follow a wrong turn, click the previous term in the chain to go back, or click *HOME* to go the Yahoo! homepage.

5 Alternatively, you can click the *BACK* button. Do that here and go back to the WWW section, then click *SEARCHING THE WEB*.

6 This takes you to a page that features more categories – from All-in-One Search Pages to Web Directories and Weblogs. By each heading is a number that tells you how many links are in that section.

7 Click *INDICES TO WEB DOCUMENTS* and you access a page with more categories (Best of the Web to What's New) along with a general list of links to different types of web index sites.

8 Incidentally, at the top of each page, there's a search engine that lets you search the whole web, UK sites or just sites in the particular category you're investigating.

Good online directories are like well-designed libraries. In real-world libraries, you often arrive at a shelf stacked with scores of titles relating to a particular field. Unless you know beforehand the title you're after, the only way to find out if a book is suitable is to have a look. Similarly, when you're faced with thirty links to sites offering to tell you 'What's New on the Web', the only way to find out more is to click the links and have a look. And that can be a bit hit-and-miss. Yahoo! is great at cataloguing sites, but it isn't in the business of quality control. A slightly different, more personal approach is offered by About.com **http://www.about.com**. Here, various human reviewers are responsible for covering a particular area and offering tips and reviews about the best sites. There are lots of directories that focus on a particular subject, or cater to a particular group of users. You can find out what's available via Directory Guide **http://www.directoryguide.com** and Search Engine Guide **http://www.searchengineguide.com**. As you might expect, there are lots of specialist kids' directories. You can find out more about them on page 205.

For less precise searching, try web rings, which are loose collectives of sites all devoted to the same basic subject, usually put up by fans and amateurs. In a web ring, sites are connected, so that you can move from one to the other by clicking the Next Site link at the bottom of a page. Alternatively, the starting-point of the ring usually offers a link to a master list of all the sites involved. There are web rings devoted to all sorts of subjects – from Afro-American issues **http://www.soulsearch.net/aawr/results.html** to the 'Rugrats' TV show **http://www.geocities.com/Hollywood/Set/9404/webring.html**. Try Yahoo! Webring **http://dir.webring.yahoo.com/rw** for a guide to existing rings and help with starting one of your own.

Weblogs Weblogs are collections of links to different sites/pages. They're put up mostly by ordinary users, updated on a regular basis and often focused on a particular subject. They can be a great way to keep up with the latest on a particular subject. There are several weblogs devoted to pointing you to the latest quality writing online – for example Arts and Letters Daily **http://www.aldaily.com** and the *Guardian's* own weblog **http://www.guardian.co.uk/weblog**. Why not give them a try? Remember, the web is for you as well as your kids.

Downloading files from the net

A few years ago, to download files from the net you needed an FTP program. The letters stand for File Transfer Protocol, something which enables you to shift files around a network – either uploading them to another computer or downloading them to your hard drive. The files you wanted to download were stored on an FTP site – a sort of online file library. These days, pretty much everything you need is on the web and you can access it via your browser. Just click on the appropriate link and after a while you'll have something potentially useful/entertaining on your hard drive.

How downloading can benefit your family:

- Go to the right places online and you can download software programs, music files, video clips, animations, demo versions of video games, even text versions of classic novels. Many of them will be available free of charge.

- Children can download screensavers, computer wallpaper and more related to their favourite bands, TV shows and toys.

- You can download upgrades and patches for your favourite pieces of software (a patch is a small file that fixes a bug/problem in a program, or tweaks some of its basic features).

Potential problems with downloading that parents need to be aware of:

- Many of the free things you can download from the net come with hidden costs of various kinds (not necessarily financial). More on this shortly.

- Software downloaded from the net can be a source of computer viruses. Always virus-check it before you install it and check out the credentials of the site you download it from.

- Old-style FTP sites are still around. In fact, fly-by-night FTP sites are used to distribute pirated software, games and other illegal/dodgy stuff (everything from bootleg music files to porn). As a result, some net gurus suggest you should keep children away from FTP sites. If your teenagers start spending a lot of time on FTP sites, don't immediately assume they're up to something. They might just be downloading freely available software. Ask them before you jump to conclusions.

How free is free software?

Many of the programs/files online can be downloaded for free. Shakespeare plays, customized levels from computer games, all sorts of software – if you don't count your telephone charges, you can get them all without handing over any money. There are some idealistic souls who do give away things online without wanting something back. But most people who give you things for free are expecting something back – your ongoing loyalty, your personal information, your attention in general. There are three basic types of free software you're likely to find yourself downloading.

- **Freeware** You don't have to pay anything for this, though sometimes the creators ask for a kind of forfeit. You might be asked to send them a postcard of where you live. There are fully-fledged freeware programs, but often many commercial software companies also release free patches.

- **Shareware** One of the more misunderstood terms in computer culture. Shareware is actually a 'try before you buy' product: you're supposed to use an evaluation copy of a program for a given period, and when that's over, you have to register it and pay something if you want to keep using it. Some pieces of shareware 'time out': you can't use them after a certain point. Others continue to work, but with certain features disabled. The makers can't force you to pay up if you continue to use their program, but they rely on you being honest. So, if you like a program, you really should pay your shareware fees. Plus, shareware is a clever way of keeping software prices down. It bypasses the regular commercial channels and their built-in overheads. And it only works if everyone plays the game.

- **Beta versions** These are test versions of software currently in development and due for eventual commercial release. Betas let you see what's coming, but you also have to put up with bugs and crashes. Some betas time out after a given period. Companies don't charge for them, but neither do they offer technical support. Some run competitions in which you can pick up rewards for identifying bugs.

- **Adware** With some free products, you pay in terms of personal information or attention. Adware programs either bombard you with ads while you use them or, more insidiously, collect information about what you do online, information which is then sold on to all sorts of marketers (this is known as spyware). These programs can be prone to crashes.

Open Source

Some idealistic programmers believe that 'real' free software is about more than money and marketing. Free software is open, they say. Its source code (the stuff that makes it run) is freely available and can be modified by other programmers. If they find a problem with a free program, they can mess around with the code, come up with a solution and pass their new, improved version on to other users. The result, say enthusiasts, is that where it has a chance to flourish, this kind of free software ends up being more reliable than commercial alternatives. This sounds great. But for the moment, it's more of a techy thing. Ordinary punters don't usually have the ability or the desire to fool around with source code. That said, the Free Software movement – or rather the Open Source movement, as many now prefer to call it – is becoming more influential.

As the net is increasingly dominated by business, Open Source has become the repository for the idealism about individual empowerment and collective effort that used to cluster around the net in general. It's been described as the net's first political movement. Most of the attention now focuses on Linux, the free operating system developed in part by Linus Torvalds. Again, this isn't really for beginners. But, even if you don't want to use the software, reading about it and the political/economic issues it raises can be fascinating. If you're looking for a way to channel the energies of a computer/net-mad teenager, you could do a lot worse than point them towards the Open Source movement. A good introduction to the whole area is the Free Software Project, a website set up by the American webzine (web magazine) Salon **http://www.salon.com/tech/fsp/index.html**. Salon contributor Andrew Leonard is currently writing a book about Open Source, and in the spirit of his subject, he's making chapters available for comment prior to official publication.

Getting started

Internet Explorer 5.x or Netscape 6 are fine for most people's downloading needs. Before you get started, spend some time sorting out your computer so you know where to put all those files. Create directories/folders on your hard drive called Download and Program Files. When you download a file, stick it in the Download directory/folder.

Downloading files

Start your browser and go to WinZip **http://www.winzip.com**. To speed up download times, files are often 'compressed' into a smaller form – known as archives. Before you can use them, you need to decompress them. WinZip is the leading compression/decompression program for the PC. It's very useful, and you can get an evaluation copy from the website. Mac users should go to Aladdin Systems **http://www.aladdinsys.com** where they can get versions of Stuffit/Stuffit Expander, programs which will decompress/compress Macintosh files.

1 Once the page comes up, click on the *DOWNLOAD EVALUATION VERSION* link.

2 On the Download page, look for the link to the appropriate program for your machine (Windows 95/98/NT or Windows 3.1). Click on that and the download process will start.

3 A dialog box will come up asking whether you want to *OPEN* the file or *SAVE* it. Pick the latter.

4 You then have to specify where you want to save the file. Pick the Download directory you created, then click *SAVE*. The program will begin downloading.

5 Once it's done, yet another dialog box will appear telling you so. Click *OK*.

> **Parasite programs** When you're downloading a program, look out for additional bits of software bundled with the thing you actually want. Sometimes you can find yourself downloading spyware programs that track what you do online and sell the data to net marketers. Some companies say they have to include these programs to subsidize the development of the software you actually want. You may not mind. But before you download something, try to find out what it does and whether you can avoid having it.

Sometimes you lose your connection in the middle of a lengthy download. Both Netscape and Internet Explorer let you resume downloads – i.e. log back on and pick up where you left off. Incidentally, during a long download you don't have to wait around doing nothing. You can open a new browser window and get on the web.

Working with downloaded files

So your Download directory is now bulging with all sorts of different files. These will have different extensions. A file extension is a group of letters that come after the file name and identify what type of file it is. Most likely, you'll have a selection of **.exe**, **.zip** and **.txt** files. These are all easy to deal with.

- Just click on a **.txt** file and an application on your computer should open it for you.

- Files with the **.exe** extension are PC-executable files.

  1 First run a virus check. Always virus-check **.exe** files you get from the net before you install them.

  2 If everything is fine, just click on the file and it should unpack itself automatically.

  3 Setup will kick in and you'll be asked where you want to install the program.

  4 Pick your Program File's directory.

- **.zip** archives are collections of files that have been compressed using WinZip or something similar.

  1 You need to 'unzip' these archives before you can work with them. Get yourself the latest version of WinZip at **http://www.winzip.com**. This will be an **.exe** file, so it should be easy enough to install.

  2 Then check out the Help files for directions on how to unzip the files.

Mac users will come across some different extensions.

- Files with the **.sea** extension are self-extracting archives – the Mac equivalent of **.exe** files.

  1 Remember to virus check a **.sea** file before you install it.

  2 If it seems fine, just click on it and it should unpack itself

- Archives compressed on the Mac using Stuffit come with the extension **.sit**. You'll see a fair amount of them.

  1 To deal with these, you'll need to get Stuffit/Stuffit Expander from Aladdin Systems **http://www.aladdinsys.com**.

  2 Once you've installed Stuffit/Stuffit Expander, look in the help files for directions on decompressing your files.

You're most likely to come across **.exe** and **.zip** online, if only because PC users are in a majority on the net. However, there are lots of other file types available online. If you're puzzled by a particular file-type you or your kids have downloaded, you'll find some advice on what it is and what programs you need to handle it at the Extensions Encyclopedia at the File Format site **http://fileformat.virtualave.net/ext_a.htm**.

Finding files on the net

If you're looking for software, try the 'software warehouse' websites. Here are a few to be getting on with:

Download.com **http://download.cnet.com/**
Shareware.com **http://shareware.cnet.com/**
Stroud's **http://cws.internet.com**
Tucows **http://www.tucows.com**

Many software warehouses have special kids' sections where you'll find all sorts of goodies. Alternatively, have a look at:

Family Games **http://www.familygames.com**
Kids Domain Downloads **http://www.kidsdomain.com/down**
Kids Freeware **http://www.kidsfreeware.com**

Downloading from the software warehouses

Once you find a piece of software you need at one of the 'software warehouses', you'll be directed to a site where you can download the program in question; usually it will be the site maintained by the company responsible for the program. When you get there, you may be offered the choice of downloading from a local mirror site – a copy of the site maintained at another computer, usually on a different continent. The idea is to find somewhere less busy and save download time. So how do you pick the right mirror site?

- Don't immediately pick the nearest UK site. Trying to download something from a British site during early evening peak time would be asking for trouble.

- Find a site in a part of the world that's asleep, and hence unlikely to be online.

- Alternatively, pick a site in a country that's unlikely to have a huge net population.

- US sites can be fine if you're downloading in the morning, UK time, when most Americans should be asleep.

Finding the free/trial version When you visit a site to download a program, you sometimes have to hunt around a bit to find the free/trial version of the software. Often the company behind the product foregrounds the links to the commercial versions of the program, generally labelled 'Gold' or 'Extra', and hides the more basic versions. You can't blame them, I guess. And if you like a program, it can be worth buying the commercial version, which usually comes with lots of extra features. But don't be conned into paying to download a 'Gold' version before you've tried out the more basic free program.

File-sharing

One of the reasons teenagers used FTP sites in the past was to download their favourite music, in the form of MP3 files, many of which had been created illegally. Getting music this way, though free of charge, was hard work. The sites featuring bootleg MP3 files often disappeared after a few hours, to avoid music industry watchdogs. And when you did find a functioning site, it often featured a rather limited selection of tracks. Things changed with the arrival in autumn 1999 of Napster **http://www.napster.com**. Designed by nineteen-year-old Shawn Fanning, Napster in its original form was a free file-sharing network that made it easy for people to swap MP3s stored on their own hard drives. First you installed the Napster software, then logged on to the Napster network. When you searched for a particular track, Napster searched the hard drives of everyone else logged on to the network to see if they had what you wanted. It then showed a list of results. Downloading a particular MP3 was just a matter of clicking on a link. Once downloaded, the file was stored in your Napster directory and made available for others to download whenever you were online and logged on to Napster. Hence file-sharing.

At its most popular, Napster had over fifty million users worldwide, and because so many people were using it, it was easy to find all sorts of music on it. Some MP3 files were available via Napster because the artists and record companies behind them had put them there. But most of the files people shared were there illegally. The artists and record companies received no money as their music moved around the net. So it was only a matter of time before they acted. After various lawsuits, Napster went offline at the start of summer 2001. By the time you read this, it may have re-launched in its new more industry-friendly format. Fans will apparently pay a subscription to use the service and the files they trade will use new encryption technologies to prevent illegal copying. This new Napster is only one of several music subscription services due to launch shortly. MusicNet, PressPlay and FullAudio are all on the way. Each is tied to a particular big record label and technology company. The files they offer will come with various encryption technologies to prevent illegal copying by the people who download them.

It's not hard to see why Napster took off. Most people want to listen to more music than they can afford. Napster let them. It also let them listen to music with a new flexibility. They weren't tied to buying a whole CD to get the two tracks they actually liked. Of course, they weren't tied to buying anything with Napster. So were Napster users breaking the law? Strictly speaking, yes. However, when so many people break a law, it's a sign that it might need rethinking. That was the argument put forward by Napster champions, who said that, rather than demonizing its customers, the big record companies should have found ways to respond to their desires. Many Napster users often went on to buy CDs by the bands they sampled via the service, they argued. So the music business should have seen the service as a form of advertising. Some bands did. Radiohead released their last two CDs on to the net for fans to trade, and the resulting buzz has been credited with getting the albums to the top of the charts and selling out their subsequent American tour.

In a way, arguments about Napster might seem a little academic now. After all, the service is now going legit. However, its place has been taken by new services that either reproduce and extend the free file-sharing idea or give users new ways of finding music files online. The best known are:

Aimster http://www.aimster.com

BearShare http://www.bearshare.com

FreeNet http://freenet.sourceforge.net

Gnutella http://gnutella.wego.com

KaZaA http://www.kazaa.com

LimeWire http://www.limewire.com

Morpheus http://www.musiccity.com

WinMX http://www.winmx.com

These services aren't exclusively devoted to swapping music files. Freenet is about using the net to help dissidents route round repressive regimes and circulate information and ideas anonymously. However, this move beyond music may present a problem for parents. If your kids used Napster, they may have been breaking the law. But, looking at it cynically, they had safety in numbers: the rest of the world was doing it too, so they were highly unlikely to find themselves in court. Crucially, when using Napster, they were only exposed to music. On the other services, along with music, your kids might find online copies of big Hollywood movies and various kinds of pornographic content, amongst other things.

So if your teenage kids are massive music fans who listen to a lot of music via the computer, it's worth keeping an eye on what they get up to. Look out for software created by the above companies being installed on the computer. Lots of new companies are popping up in this area – you can keep up with what's going on via ZeroPaid http://www.zeropaid.com, which reviews the various file-sharing services. If your child does start using one of these services a lot, it's not necessarily a bad thing. It's not something you need to get heavy about. A better strategy might be to talk about what they do on the service, what files they download, the copyright issues and how it impacts on their favourite artists. You might be surprised at the sophistication of their responses.

Parasite programs and file-sharing Some of the most popular file-sharing services come with the kinds of parasite programs mentioned before, spyware that tracks what you do and finds new ways to target ads at you while you're online. At the time of writing, KaZaA in particular comes with a lot of extra plug-ins and programs that do all sorts of things you might not be happy about. See if you can opt out of these before you download the main program.

In fact, if you're looking to channel the energies of a computer-mad teenager, this area might come in handy. Behind these file sharing services lies a big new net idea – peer to peer networking, or P2P, as jargonauts call it. Net idealists have worried for some time now that the net is becoming too corporate, too centralized and too commercial. File sharing networks seem to be a move in the other direction. They do the thing the net was always supposed to do – let ordinary people communicate with each other, without central control. Hence peer to peer networking.

P2P lets people pool the power they have in their desktop PCs to achieve different things. Napster worked by aggregating the disk space on individual users' PCs to create an enormous online storage system. You can also pool the unused processing power of individual computers to create a huge, distributed supercomputer. SETI@Home **http://setiathome.ssl.berkeley.edu/**

uses distributed computing to analyse radio signals from space for evidence of alien communication. Parabon **http://www.parabon.com** is using distributed computing power for research into cancer cures. There's lots of interesting work being done in the area, work that may fire the imagination of idealistic teenagers. To find out more, try O'Reilly's OpenP2P **http://openp2p.com/**. The page put up by American net guru Clay Shirky **http://www.shirky.com** also has lots of interesting thoughts about P2P and more.

Web multimedia

When it first started, the web was just text and still graphics. That seemed pretty radical at the time. Now, of course, the web is a full-blown multimedia experience. The video is small screen and rather scratchy. You have to wait for those online cartoons and interactive interfaces to load. Of course, sometimes it isn't worth the wait. But while you might be happy just reading while you're online, your children won't be. They'll want all the multimedia the web can throw at them.

How web multimedia can benefit your family:

- Children can listen to music and watch video clips (everything from pop videos to film trailers).

- They can watch online cartoons and play games that feature their favourite film/TV characters.

- They can see what's happening on the other side of the world, courtesy of live webcams set up in places of interest.

- Music-mad teens can personalize online radio stations so that they only hear the bands they like.

Potential problems with web multimedia that parents need to be aware of:

- A lot of the multimedia content is aimed at the 18-25 age range. In particular many of the short films and cartoons you find online deal in gross/sick humour and are deliberately near the knuckle. They're often very funny. But they're probably not the kind of thing you want your ten-year-olds watching just yet.

- Lots of the sites that feature links to different webcams around the world also have links to some of the webcams that feature pornographic content.

As ever, the best thing is to keep a discreet eye on the sites your kids like to visit online and talk to them about the pages they visit. And, if you want to take things further, there are programs you can install to keep your children away from this kind of stuff. You'll find out more on page 254.

Older computers To enjoy web multimedia, the old PC you bought five years ago really won't do. The minimum you need is a soundcard, a good graphics/video card with at least 2MB of memory (more will make video look better), a reasonably speedy processor and a 56.6Kbps modem.

Using your browser to access multimedia

A few years ago, you needed to augment your browser with special booster programs known as plug-ins if you wanted to access the various types of online multimedia. At first, there were lots of competing plug-ins. Now, a few programs (generally known as media players or image viewers) have pretty much cornered the market. These are the players/viewers you'll need.

• **RealNetworks' RealPlayer** This handles streaming audio/video/animation (the files play as you download them, so you don't need to wait until they're completely downloaded). Your browser should come with this pre-installed. If it doesn't, or you want to get the latest version, visit Real Networks' UK website at **http://uk.real.com** – RealPlayer Basic is the free player.

- **Macromedia's Shockwave and Flash Players** The standard tools for interactive multimedia and animated graphics on the web. Again, both should already be installed in the browser you get from your ISP. If they aren't, or you want to update them, go to Macromedia **http://www.macromedia.com/shockwave/**. Both are free.

There are other programs you can use to handle audio/video:

- **Windows Media Player** Now bundled with Internet Explorer, this does most of the things RealPlayer does.

- **Apple's QuickTime** This handles sound and 3-D visuals as well as video – download it from **http://www.apple.com/quicktime/**.

When it comes to playing music online, in particular using MP3 music files, you have other options too:

- **RealNetworks' RealJukebox** A music player you can use to play music files, record music you've downloaded from the web onto CDs, create playlists, listen to online radio stations and more. It's available at **http://www.real.com/jukebox/index.html**.

- **WinAmp** A very popular music player that handles most MPEG audio files, specifically MP3s. It's available at **http://www.winamp.com**.

There are other types of viewers/players that will come in handy online. Here's a couple you might enjoy:

- **Adobe Acrobat Reader** This will let you read documents created using Adobe's Acrobat graphics program – specifically files with the **.pdf** extension. Lots of official government documents are available in this format, including Ofsted school reports. Download it from **http://www.adobe.com/products/acrobat/readstep.html**.

- **Paint Shop Pro** Digital photography is becoming more and more popular. There are all sorts of programs you can get that let you both view and manipulate your photos on your computer. This is one of the best – download it from **http://www.jasc.com**.

Web photo services If photography is your thing, you might enjoy the web services that let you store your snaps online and share them with others. If you use a digital camera, you can upload your shots directly to a password-protected area on the web, where friends/family can browse them. If you use standard film, many sites will now develop your shots, then display them online for friends to see. Some sites then let you choose to have the best shots developed as prints. Incidentally, some American sites also offer picture-editing tools that let you crop/cut out red eye etc online. The leading British sites are: Boots Photo **http://www.bootsphoto.com**, Fotango **http://www.fotango.com** and Uboot **http://www.uboot.com/uk/cheez/**. Yahoo! UK also runs a similar service at **http://uk.photos.yahoo.com/**.

Accessing web media is pretty easy. When you come across a particular type of media content on a webpage, just click on it. The media player that came with your browser will start up and play the file in question. As mentioned before, Netscape 6 and Internet Explorer 5 come with RealPlayer and Shockwave pre-installed. Sometimes you might encounter a problem if the media file has been designed for the latest version of a particular player. However most websites that feature multi-media content provide links to the appropriate version of the viewer/player. Incidentally, Netscape 6 makes it easy to check which players you have and what versions they are. Select the *HELP* menu, then *ABOUT PLUG-INS* and you'll see a handy list.

Microsoft introduced its own way of handling certain types of web multimedia – Active X. ActiveX controls are a bit like plug-ins in that they are integrated with your browser and enable it to play multimedia within its main window. If you're using Internet Explorer and you come across a page that uses an ActiveX control you haven't got, your browser will start to download it. It may flash up a Security Warning screen to check that it's OK. Be very wary of downloading Active X controls from sites you're not familiar with or that don't appear to be reputable.

There are all sorts of other booster programs and plug-ins you can use to either handle media files or help with other browsing tasks. They're sometimes referred to as browsing companions, helper applications/helper apps, utilities or add-ons. To see just how many are available, visit CNet's browsers section **http://www.cnet.com/internet/0-3773.html** and look for their browsing companions directory. New plug-ins and add-ons appear all the time. Sometimes, thanks to the habit of adding extra 'parasite' programs to certain sought-after downloads (detailed previously on page XX), all sorts of odd little bits of software can find their way onto your computer if you're not careful.

Try to keep an eye out for so-called 'scumware' plug-ins, which have recently been causing concern among groups devoted to protecting kids on the net. These allow keywords on any webpage to become advertising links. Once you move your cursor over a keyword, a set of links to supposedly relevant sites is revealed. This could be useful, though there is some evidence it's being used in some cases to advertise porn/gambling sites. So a web site might feature the word 'love', which, if you've installed a particular plug-in, will become a link to various adult sites that have paid the plug-in makers for the privilege. Other plug-ins replace the banner ads on a page with other ads selected by the plug-in makers. Again, there is concern that these ads might be for adult sites. At the moment, the programs

causing most concern are eZula's TopText, Filemix's Surf+ and Gator's Offer Companion, but others may appear. You can keep up with new developments at
http://www.freegraphics.com/zz-scumware/.

BonziBuddy Your kids may enjoy this rather literal spin on the idea of a browsing companion. Bonzi is a purple cartoon gorilla who, once installed on your desktop, accompanies you as you surf, offering suggestions about other links, cracking jokes and so on. Download it from
http://www.bonzi.com/bonzibuddy/bonzibuddyfreehom.asp.

Email

Even those who hate the net generally make an exception where email is concerned. It's now an accepted part of our lives, and it's not hard to see why it has caught on. For the cost of a local telephone call (or less), you can quickly send messages to someone on the other side of the world. You can send more than just plain text – attaching image and sound files to mail is easy. And for no extra cost, you can send mail to lots of people at the same time. Email makes it easier to stay in touch with family, friends and business colleagues abroad. Thanks to web-mail and the spread of cybercafes, it's becoming the preferred way of staying in touch with home while you're travelling for business or pleasure.

However, there's more to email than speed and convenience. Perhaps because it sits somewhere between speech and writing, because it's like a letter with the immediacy of a telephone call, it seems to encourage directness and intimacy, though this can cut both ways. Friendships have been built – and broken – by email. It's so easy to press *SEND* that people often do it before they engage their brains. They fire off angry replies to messages intended as jokes (tone and sarcasm are hard to transmit over the wires). They send friends messages meant for others. In general, email's ease of use means that our online mailboxes are packed with messages, most of them spam (online junk mail). You don't just need to learn how to send and receive email. You also need to learn how to cope with it – and the same goes for your kids.

How email can benefit your family:

- It's a great way to stay in touch with relatives.

- As kids get older they may use it instead of the phone to contact their friends (though don't bank on it – chat and instant messaging seems to be the modern teenager's preferred mode of communication).

- Both parents and kids can sign up to their favourite sites and receive regular free updates about things they're interested in.

- Children can join online pen pal programs and exchange mail with kids from around the world.

Potential problems with email that parents need to be aware of:

- Children may take offence at mail that wasn't actually intended to hurt. They may also give offence via an email message when they didn't mean to. Adult friends have fallen out over email – it can happen with kids too.

- Sending deliberately threatening/insulting mail is becoming something of a favourite teenage prank. The people doing this usually don't realize how much it hurts. But when abusive mail turns up on your own computer, it can feel like an invasion of your own private space.

- Viruses that spread via email attachments can be a particular problem for kids. They often open attachments first and think later.

- The same goes for spam, especially from porn sites. Often the people sending this stuff to your kids don't realize who they're sending it to. They use software to 'harvest' addresses from the net. They may have found your child's address from a personal web site or a discussion board or an online profile. To them, it's just another address. To you and your kids, it's something rather different.

• Some people do deliberately seek out children's addresses, often with the hope of exploiting email's intimacy to their own ends – everyone from dubious marketing types to online predators. This doesn't happen that often, but the potential is there. For that reason, if you do give your kids their own personal email addresses, you need to think carefully about keeping those addresses private.

What software do you need?

All you need really is your web browser. Netscape 6 and Internet Explorer both come with mail packages. You'll find the Netscape 6 Mail program in the *TASKS* menu.

The IE mail program is called Outlook Express. Both are now as good as most of the specialist mail programs. If you have the disk space, you could install both and switch between them to see which you prefer. However, you will have to nominate one as your default, so that when you click an email link on a webpage (for example, to send mail to the person responsible for the page), the computer knows which program to start up.

The Mac version of Outlook Express is slightly different. It's still easy enough to figure out, but where there might be potential for confusion I've tried to include specific instructions for Mac users of Outlook Express. If you want a specialist mail program, go for Eudora **http://www.eudora.com**.

Configuring Your mail software

The mail program that came with the browser supplied by your ISP may have been configured during the general installation process. However, if you're installing something from scratch, you'll need to enter a few details before you can send any mail.

You may have to enter any and all of the following:

YOUR NAME: As in Jim McClellan.

YOUR EMAIL ADDRESS: Your ISP will have given you this when you signed on – something like **yourname@yourserviceprovider.net** (or, depending on the ISP, **.com** or **.co.uk**).

YOUR RETURN EMAIL ADDRESS: Usually the same as above, though you can enter something different if you're going to be picking up replies at another location (e.g. work).

YOUR USER NAME (ALSO KNOWN AS THE ACCOUNT NAME): The first part of your email address – i.e. **jim.mcclellan**.

OUTGOING MAIL SERVER (SMTP): The computer at your ISP that handles the mail you send to other people. This will usually be something like **mail.yourserviceprovider.net**.

INCOMING MAIL SERVER (POP3): The computer that handles the mail other people send you. Again, this will be something like **mail.yourserviceprovider.net**.

PASSWORD: The password your ISP gave you when you signed up.

- **To configure Outlook Express:**
  1 The first time you use it, the *INTERNET CONNECTION WIZARD* should take you through the configuration process.
  2 If it doesn't, start it up by selecting the *TOOLS* menu, then *ACCOUNTS*. Click the *ADD* button, then *MAIL*. Then you can enter the required information.
  3 If you need to change existing account information (you might change ISPs and email address), pick your account then click on *PROPERTIES*.

- **To configure Netscape 6 Mail:**
  1 First open *MAIL*, via the *TASKS MENU*.
  2 Select *EDIT*, then *MAIL / NEWS ACCOUNT SETTINGS*.
  3 Click on the *NEW ACCOUNT* button. The *ACCOUNT WIZARD* will start up and guide you through configuration.

- **To configure the Mac version of Outlook Express:**
  1 Select the *TOOLS* menu, then *ACCOUNTS*, then *MAIL*.
  2 With a new Mac/iMac, you can do this via the *APPLE* menu. Select *CONTROL PANELS*, then *INTERNET*. This brings up a dialog box where you can enter details about your email account.

Screen names and children I've mentioned this before, but it's worth repeating as we start to look at communicating online. Children should use non-gender specific screen names, based on things like their interests rather than their real-world identity. This becomes very important when children use chatrooms or discussion boards. The idea is to avoid hassles from the troglodyte males (and worse) who populate some online spaces.

Your first message

Now's the time for you and your kids to annoy friends and family with those 'Hey, we're online, finally' messages. (To really wind them up, call them repeatedly to see whether they've got your mail yet.) If you want to avoid family feuds, why not send a message to the *Guardian* instead. We've set up a program that automatically replies to all mail you and your kids send to **guidetest@guardian.co.uk**. It may be a touch impersonal, but it will let you check whether your first mail reached its destination.

1 Open your mail program and click the *NEW MESSAGE / COMPOSE MESSAGE* button. A window will open that is split into two parts. The bottom part is where you write your message; the top part is where you write the address and the subject.

2 Click in the *TO:* field to move the cursor there, then enter the address – **guidetest@guardian.co.uk** – don't add an extra full stop at the end – however they may appear in the media (or in this book), email addresses do not end in full stops. If all this looks rather confusing, go back to page 42 for more information.

3 Your own address may already be in the *FROM:* field. In the *SUBJECT:* field, put a brief description of your message – *My First Message* or some such. Pretty soon you'll discover how useful the *SUBJECT:* field is and you'll curse people who don't bother entering anything there. Ignore the other fields in this window for the moment.

4 Click in the bottom part of the window and write your mail. What you put here is obviously up to you.

··

Email style

··

None of what you may have learnt at school about laying out letters really applies to email.

• You don't need to write your address in the top right-hand corner. When people get your email, their mailbox will show them who sent it and what it's about (if you enter something in the *SUBJECT:* field).

• Some people don't bother opening their mail with a 'Dear Jim' and just get straight to the message.

• Email purists also don't sign off with a 'Yours, Dave' or whatever, but instead include a personal 'signature file', aka 'sig file'. This usually contains your contact details – name, email address, perhaps real-world address and telephone number(s) – plus a jokey/deep quotation that shows what a deep/sexy individual you are.

• If you do use a sig file, think about the recipient of your message. Do you want them to have all your contact details? Creating sig files for your children needs extra care too.

Your mail package will let you compose a signature file and save it. When you write mail, you will be able to paste it in automatically at the end of the message.

• **In Outlook Express:**

  1 Select the *TOOLS* menu, then *OPTIONS*, then the *SIGNATURES* tab.

  2 You can then compose your signature and choose to add it to all messages.

• **In Netscape 6 Mail:**

  1 Compose your signature in your word processor program and save it.

  2 Select *EDIT*, then *PREFERENCES*, then *MAIL / NEWS ACCOUNT SETTINGS*.

3 On the *ACCOUNT SETTINGS* box, put a tick next to *ATTACH* this signature.

4 Click the *CHOOSE* button to find the file you created. Then click *OK*.

- **In the Mac version of Outlook Express:**

  1 Select the *TOOLS* menu, then *SIGNATURES*.

  2 When you compose a new message, there's a *SIGNATURE* toolbar you can use to add your sig file to the message.

Remember that these layout conventions are optional. If you want your email to be like your real-world mail, fine. The only principle you should stick to is to keep things brief wherever possible. People are paying to download your mail, so the idea is not to add to their bills, in however minuscule a way. Here are a few other things to remember when writing your email.

- Perhaps because it's somewhere between speech and writing, email tends to be more informal and slangy than real-world mail. In theory, you don't need to take quite as much care with your grammar and upper/lower cases. That said, sending illiterate pieces of doggerel isn't good email style either.

- You can compress messages even further by using TLAs, as in Three-Letter Acronyms. This includes things like WRT – with regards to, IMO – in my opinion, OTOH – on the other hand.

- Capitals are used for emphasis in email – they're the online equivalent of shouting. Shy away from them unless you really need to make a point. It can look rather rude and people do get the hump.

- You can also use emoticons or smileys (little sideways-on faces constructed from keyboard characters) to indicate emotion: :-) means happy; :-(indicates sadness, and ;-) is supposed to signal irony. It can be hard to interpret the tone or spirit of a piece of mail, especially if it's supposed to be funny or sarcastic. Smileys, which supply the kind of facial cues you'd get if you were talking face to face, are supposed to help. They're very popular with kids, less so with those over the age of consent, though there are exceptions. Netscape 6 is now set by default to display the more common smileys as cartoon graphics. If you want to turn this off, select *EDIT*, then *PREFERENCES*, then click on *MESSAGE DISPLAY* (it's in the Mail and Newsgroups section) and untick the appropriate box.

TLAs and smileys For a pretty comprehensive list of smileys and TLAs (and a useful glossary of general net jargon), try Netlingo at **http://www.netlingo.com**.

HTML or plain text mail?

Email used to be just plain text (known as ASCII). But now there's also HTML mail, which means letters with pictures, links and more. Most new mail programs automatically send HTML mail unless you tell them otherwise. Some older mail programs may have difficulties with this. If you send HTML mail to someone whose software can't handle it, it will appear in their inbox as text plus an attached HTML file. If you think there might be a problem, check that the person you're mailing can receive HTML mail. If they can't, send plain text.

- In Outlook Express:
  1 Open a *NEW MESSAGE* window.
  2 Select the *FORMAT* menu, then either *PLAIN TEXT* or *RICH TEXT* (HTML).

- **With Netscape 6 Mail:**

  1 Select *EDIT* then *MAIL / NEWS ACCOUNT SETTINGS*. At the bottom of the *ACCOUNT SETTINGS* dialog box, either tick or untick the box next to *COMPOSE MESSAGES IN HTML FORMAT*.

  2 Alternatively, select *EDIT*, then *PREFERENCES*, then *SEND FORMAT* – it's in the *MAIL AND NEWS* section. You can then choose to automate the whole process of choosing formats in various ways.

Sending your first message

You've written your message to the *Guardian* and you're happy with it:

  1 To send it straight away, just get online then press the *SEND* button.

  2 Alternatively, you can stay offline and choose to send your mail later. It will be transferred to your *OUTBOX* or *UNSENT MAIL* folder, depending on which mail program you're using.

  3 You can then write more messages and stack them up in the *OUTBOX* to send them all at once.

  4 If you close your mail program without sending your mail, you may get a brief reminder asking whether you want to send it now.

  5 With unsent or queued mail, most mail software will send it automatically the next time you check your own mail.

  6 Most mail software is set up to save a copy of mail you send, usually in the *OUTBOX* or in the *SENT ITEMS* folder.

After you've sent your mail to **guidetest@guardian.co.uk**, if everything's working, you should get a reply from us in a couple of hours.

TROUBLESHOOTING

Occasionally, email might be bounced back to you unsent.

- Usually, the problem is caused by errors in the address. Check the spelling and make sure you haven't added spaces or extra periods.

- If everything seems in order, the person you're mailing may have changed address.

- Alternatively, the problem may be at the ISP where your intended recipient has his or her mailbox. Their computers may be down – in which case, try sending your message later.

Getting your mail

Email sent to you sits in your mailbox on your ISP's mail server until you collect it. To pick up your mail:

- **In Outlook Express,** click *SEND AND RECEIVE*.

- **In Netscape 6 Mail,** click the *GET MESSAGE* button

Once you do:

1 You'll be connected to the net and your messages will be downloaded. Once you've got them all, log off.

2 A window may open showing the new mail in your Inbox. If not, click on your *INBOX* icon or button.

3 For each piece of new mail, you'll see a line of information, telling you who sent it and when and what it's about. Double-click on that and the message will open in a new window.

Multiple identities Outlook Express lets you create a different 'identity' for each person that uses it. Each user can then maintain separate messages, contacts, and personal settings. To create a new identity, select the *FILE* menu, then *IDENTITIES*, then *ADD NEW IDENTITY*. You can also choose to password this. To switch to a particular identity, select the *FILE* menu, then *SWITCH IDENTITY*.

Replying to your mail

A friend has emailed you and you want to reply:

1 Just click on the *REPLY TO* button.
2 This will open a *NEW MESSAGE* window with your friend's address already filled in.
3 In the *SUBJECT:* field, it will say 'Re:', followed by whatever your friend entered in the *SUBJECT* line.
4 Click in the bottom window and write your reply

When replying to mail, it can be helpful to quote from the original message. If you use the *REPLY TO* button on most mailers, when the message window opens it will display the original message indented with 'quote tags', as in:

>Jim
>blah blah blah
>Wally

You can then edit this, selecting the bits you want to keep and adding your own contributions, as in:

On 10 March, Wally wrote
>blah blah blah
See what you mean, Wally.
Jim

The end result simulates a kind of conversation and helps to keep track of ideas over several messages. However:

- Make sure you edit the previous message so that only the appropriate bits are included.

- Don't send people a complete copy of their previous mail when replying – it can get irritating, especially if the first mail was rather long.

- In theory, you should reply to email quickly, if only to confirm you received the message. Sometimes, if a reply doesn't appear for a while, you start to wonder whether your mail actually reached its destination.

- Then again, just because email goes a lot faster, it doesn't mean you have to as well. One of the bad things about email is that it often carries a kind of implicit pressure to speed things up and write back NOW!

Reading mail offline Perhaps this sounds a bit obvious, but whenever possible, work on your mail offline. Once you've downloaded mail sent to you, disconnect and then read it, then write your reply. It's easy to forget to log off.

Carbon copies and forwarding

Email makes it easy to send the same message to groups of people. You can do this either by using carbon copy (Cc) or blind carbon copy (Bcc). If you use the Cc option, recipients will see who else got your message. If you use Bcc, they won't.

- In Outlook Express:

  1 You'll see a *CC:* line underneath the *TO:* line. Type in the addresses you want here.

  2 If you want to use the *BCC* option but can't see it, move your cursor over the *CC:* and it will turn into a button.

  3 Click on the button and you'll be able to access the *BCC:* line.

- In Netscape 6 Mail:

  1 To add *CC* and *BCC* addresses, just click the *TO:* button in the *ADDRESS* window.

It's also easy to forward mail. Once a message is open, just click the *FORWARD* button and a *NEW MESSAGE* window will open with the old message in quote tags. Then enter the address of the person you want to forward it to and add any comments.

Address books and email directories

If someone sends you mail, you can add their contact details to an address book for future reference – helpful if you find it difficult to remember email addresses or type them out without making mistakes. You can also enter more information – whether they prefer HTML mail or text, for example.

- **In Outlook Express:**

  1 Click the *ADDRESS BOOK* button.

  2 To add a new entry to the book, click the *NEW* button, then select *NEW CONTACT*.

  3 To send a message to someone, click on their name, then click the *ACTION* button and select *MAIL*.

  4 To add more information to their entry, click on their name, then the *PROPERTIES* button.

  5 Outlook Express also keeps an easy-access *CONTACTS* list on the bottom left of the screen. To write to someone on this list, double click on their name.

- **In Netscape 6 Mail:**

  1 Select the *TASKS* menu, then *ADDRESS BOOK*.

  2 To add someone to the book, select *PERSONAL* from the browser bar on the left, click the *NEW CARD* button on the toolbar, then fill out the relevant details.

  3 To send a message, click on the person's name, then click the *NEW MSG* button.

  4 To add more detail to their entry, click on the name, then the *EDIT* button.

Outlook Express lets you search various online directories for email addresses. These are a bit hit-and-miss. Some rely on sub-missions from users. Others use software that trawls the net for addresses. They all have a definite American bias. All of them will turn up plenty of results – especially if you do a simple search on a name. But you then have to figure out which, if any, might belong to the person you're trying to contact. Once you're online:

- **In Outlook Express:**

  1 Click the *ADDRESS BOOK* button, then click *FIND PEOPLE* toolbar button. A Find People dialog box will come up.

  2 Click the *LOOK IN* drop-down window to pick a directory to search, then enter the name of the person you're searching for and click the *FIND NOW* button. (This works slightly differently in the Mac version, but it's easy enough to understand.)

> **Netscape 6 and mailing lists** The address book in Netscape 6.1 Mail has a neat function that lets you assemble lists of different people you can use for mass mail-outs. Very useful for business, but also handy if you're trying to mail news to family and friends. Access the *ADDRESS BOOK* as normal, then use the *NEW LIST* button on the toolbar to create a mailing list.

Email and attachments

You can attach all sorts of different files to your messages – everything from still images to video clips and programs. Attaching files has been made easy by modern mail software.

1 In Outlook Express or Netscape 6 Mail, just click the *ATTACH* button on the toolbar (the one with the paperclip on it).

2 Find the file you want to send in your directory, then click on *ATTACH*.

3 Then send your mail as normal.

This sounds very easy, and usually it is. The difficulties that do arise are generally caused by people not checking whether recipients of their mail can cope with particular types of attachments. Problems can also be caused by Mac users sending files to PC owners and vice versa. So how do things go wrong? The files you attach to your mail are usually quite large, so your mail program converts them to make them easier to send. A few years ago, most PC mail programs converted attachments using something called UUencode. This was replaced by MIME, which is now the standard. Mac mail programs also used Bin Hex. Modern mail programs can cope with all of these. However, when it comes to email, many people are happy chugging along with the old program they've always used – until they get a chunk of indecipherable gibberish in their mailbox. So, before you send an attachment to someone:

- Find out what mail program they use. If they use a newer mailer, there should be no problem.

- If they have an old program (something that goes back four or five years), you'll have to use UUencode.

To use UUencode for attachments:

- **In Outlook Express:**
  1 Select the *TOOLS* menu, then *OPTIONS*, then the *SEND* tab.
  2 The *MAIL* sending format will be set to HTML. Click the box by *PLAIN TEXT* to change it, then click *SETTINGS*.
  3 You can then specify either MIME or UUencode.

- **In the Mac version of Outlook Express:**
  1 Select the *EDIT* menu, then *PREFERENCES*.
  2 Then select *COMPOSE* and make the changes as required.

Receiving mail with an attachment is usually problem-free.

- Both Outlook Express and Netscape 6 Mail will usually show picture attachments in the body of the message.

- Otherwise, there should be a paperclip icon at the top of the message when you open it. If you click this, the file's name will appear.

- Click this in turn and you'll be asked if you want to open it or save it.

By the way, it's usually good form to contact someone you're planning to send a big attachment to, just to warn them to expect a longer download than usual and to see whether they want it in the first place.

Mail-borne viruses Be wary of Microsoft Word attachments. They can be host to various macro-viruses. Mail-borne viruses like Melissa and the Love Bug spread by sending themselves to all the addresses they find in the contacts book on a particular machine. If you open the attachment, they infect your machine. So even if the document apparently came from a friend, check it before you open it. Make sure your kids know about this kind of thing and remind them to always check with friends before they open an unexpected attached Word file.

Managing your email

Email doesn't clutter up your office like the stuff that comes on paper. But it can get out of control. To stay on top of it:

- Try to read messages as soon as you get them and reply reasonably quickly.

- Messages in your Inbox will probably be sorted according to the date they were received. You can order them in another way – by sender, subject and so on. In Netscape 6 Mail or Outlook Express, select the *VIEW* menu, then *SORT* or *SORT BY*.

- Be ruthless when it comes to deleting messages. It's easy to save your mail, but often you don't need to.

- If you do want to keep mail, file it when you've read it. You can set up specific folders for mail from different people, organizations, mailing lists or subjects, then transfer it easily as you read it.

To create new folders, select the *FILE* menu, then *FOLDER* or *NEW FOLDER*. To file a piece of mail:

- **In Outlook Express:**
  1 Select a message, then the *EDIT* menu.
  2 Then select *MOVE TO FOLDER*.

- **In Netscape 6 Mail:**
  1 Click the *FILE* button on the toolbar.

- **In the Mac version of Outlook Express:**
  1 Select the *MESSAGE* menu, then *MOVE TO*.

You can create filters that automatically direct incoming mail into specific folders rather than the Inbox.

- **In Outlook Express:**
  1 Select the *TOOLS* Menu, then *MESSAGE RULES*.
  2 Then select *MAIL*.

- **In Netscape 6 Mail:**
  1 Select the *EDIT* menu, then *MESSAGE FILTERS*.
  2 Click on the *NEW* button to create a filter.

- **In the Mac version of Outlook Express:**
  1 Select the *TOOLS* menu, then *RULES*.
  2 Then click on *NEW RULE*.

Next you need to specify what your software should look for and what it should do with a message that fits the parameters you set. If you get a lot of mail from a particular business colleague, you can put their address in the Sender category, then arrange to transfer it to a special mailbox/folder. Alternatively, if they never say anything interesting, divert it to the trash. Outlook Express can be set up so that it won't bother to download certain messages – i.e. spam – from your ISP's mail server.

Webmail, redirection and other mail services

In the last few years, webmail – email you read and send via a webpage – has gone from being incredibly popular to being totally ubiquitous. It's not hard to see why. Webmail makes it very easy to get your mail while travelling. All you need is a computer with a connection to the web. You can also change your ISP without having to inform friends and colleagues of your new email address. You can create multiple email addresses and use them for different things. You can 'maintain your independence' from work or college, according to one Free Mail site: if you have an official mailbox at work and that's your only connection to the net, in other words, you can set up something more personal on the web. If you share an account at home and want to keep some mail private, a web mailbox is a good option. Of course, what works for you will work for your kids. Teenagers may use webmail to avoid the prying eyes of the rest of the family.

Global net cafés Webmail is a great tool for staying in touch with your children when they get old enough to go travelling. Of course, they'll need to know where the cybercafés are in the city/country they're visiting. You can do a bit of advance research together at the Internet Café Guide **http://www.netcafeguide.com/**.

Here's a list of some of the biggest webmail services:

AOL Mail **http://aolmail.aol.com**
Email.com **http://www.email.com**
Eudora Web-Mail **http://www.eudoramail.com**
Excite **http://www.excite.co.uk**
Hot Mail **http://www.hotmail.com**
iName **http://www.iname.com**
Juno **http://www.juno.com**
Lycos Communications **http://comm.lycos.com**
Mail.com **http://www.mail.com**
Net@ddress **http://www.netaddress.com**
Talk 21 **http://www.talk21.co.uk**
Yahoo! Mail **http://mail.yahoo.co.uk**

There are lots more webmail services to choose from – the Free Email Providers Guide **http://www.fepg.net/** lists 1400 different operations around the world, along with reviews and guides to the different services. Some webmail services are designed to work in tandem with your ISP mail account. Take Big Foot **http://www.bigfoot.com**, for example, where you can create an email address for life – **jim.mcclellan@bigfoot.com** or some such.

You give this to people, and any mail arriving at this address is redirected to your ISP mail account. This reduces hassle when it comes to changing ISPs.

Bigfoot and many of the other webmail sites now offer other useful services. They send you reminders when important birthdays or anniversaries are looming. When you go on holiday, many automatically send messages to people who mail you, telling them you're away. Incidentally, most ISPs now offer these kinds of services with their regular POP3 account. If you think they might be useful, ask them what they do.

Alternative webmail accounts Webmail can come in handy if you want to keep your main email account private. Set up a webmail account and make that your public address – put it on your webpage and use it to contribute to discussion groups and mailing lists. If junk mail monsters do harvest addresses from the groups you use, at least your main account will stay spam-free. This can work for kids too, though take care with the screen name they choose.

Many webmail services are targeted at business people. Others will appeal more to your kids.

- Another.com **http://www.another.com** lets you set up a mail account with a funny/topical address – as in **jim@ihatehearsay.com**.

- Funmail **http://www.funmail.com** lets you create animated messages and mail them to your friends.

- Pass This On **http://www.passthison.com** creates images and little video clips – either 'comic' or sentimental – that you can send to your friends.

- You can also send email greetings cards – many portals and online shops offer this service for free. Otherwise, try Blue Mountain **http://www.bluemountain.com**.

- Sign up with Zap Spot **http://www.zapspot.com** and they'll send you little video games via the mail.

Internet discussion groups

The net makes one-to-one communication incredibly easy. However, its real strength is many-to-many communication. After all, if you want to contact a friend, a standard paper letter will still do the job. But what about contacting a group of friends? And what about circulating the replies so that everybody can read what everybody else has said? That kind of group communication doesn't come easily to the world of paper and stamps. The net, on the other hand, was made for it. It's easy to send a message to a group of people, and it's just as easy for each group member to send their responses to everyone else. As a result, the net is home to thousands of ongoing discussions covering all sorts of subjects and bringing together all sorts of people.

How discussion groups can benefit your family:

- There are discussion groups on many of the big children's websites. It's a good way for kids to swap ideas with other kids who share their interests.

- Teenagers are often enthusiastic participants in discussion forums devoted to their particular interests. Many also set up their own private discussion forums for their friends. Many families also set up their own discussion boards.

- Parents can join forums devoted to specific parenting topics and get advice and support.

Potential problems with email that parents need to be aware of:

- Many discussion groups are adult affairs (both in terms of content and the language used) that you wouldn't want your kids to see.

- Usenet newsgroups pose particular problems. Some are used to exchange porn – by attaching images to their messages. Much of this traffic goes via the alt.binaries groups. In other groups, people circulate illegal material – everything from pirated software to child porn. Your ISP won't carry these groups. But it will carry numerous perfectly legitimate adult groups that contain material that isn't suitable for children.

- Consequently, some parents prefer to keep their kids away from Usenet as a whole. Others let older teenagers access the newsgroups. It's up to you. But if you do let you older kids access the newsgroups, you need to talk to them about what they might find there and keep a discreet eye on what they get up to.

- It can be hard to make sure that children's discussion groups are only being used by kids. You need to check the security measures taken by the sites hosting these groups. You also need to teach your kids not to give out personal information when they contribute to these groups.

- Spammers use software to harvest email addresses from online discussion groups, then bombard people with vast amounts of junk mail.

- Discussion groups can be fractious places, where discussions often get heated and sometimes turn into full-blown flame wars (flame is online slang for an abusive or insulting message). Parents need to teach their kids how to behave in discussion groups – everything from avoiding bad language to keeping discussions on track. In particular, they need to advice on how to deal with group members who get abusive.

Watch what you say Remember that most discussion groups are public forums. They're easily accessible and easily searched. In other words, the things you write might be found by someone using the net to check you out.

'Internet discussion group' is a catch-all term that covers several different forms of group communication:

- Mailing lists – sign up to these and email from list members turns up every day in your mailbox.

- Web discussion boards – these are bulletin board-like spaces on websites where you can go to read people's messages about a particular idea or theme, then add your own thoughts.

- Usenet newsgroups – these are bulletin board-style discussions circulated through a global network of news servers. Here you subscribe to a group, download the day's messages, then post back your thoughts.

Each of these groups works in roughly the same way. You send a message about a particular topic and it goes to everyone in the group. Someone responds and, over time, a kind of delayed-action discussion builds up. Each type of group has its own strengths:

- People tend to be on mailing lists because they want to be, so discussions can be fairly focused and more productive.

- Usenet newsgroups cover all sorts of subjects. Whatever you're interested in, chances are there's a newsgroup devoted to it. However, Usenet is wilder and more freewheeling than other parts of the net.

- Web discussion boards are often a great way for people to take issue with, or expand on stories written by the mainstream media. Many big content-based websites now have discussion boards, or they let readers add their thoughts to the end of certain pieces. As a result, readers can generate conversations that are both longer and more interesting than the original articles.

As you get used to the net, you'll discover which one works for you best. But they're all worth a look when you're starting out.

Discussion group netiquette

The online world has its own code of conduct, which is known as netiquette. If you follow the rules, you'll get more out of the net, and you won't get bogged down in silly arguments and worse. That counts double for your kids, so do try to teach them good netiquette. In discussion groups, it's particularly important to find out how things are done and go with the flow. If you don't, you can mess things up for everyone involved.

- When you're contributing to a discussion group, keep things brief and to the point.

- Use smileys and TLAs if they speed things up and are easily understood – and if they seem to fit the group.

- Using capitals is the equivalent of shouting and should be avoided.

- When you first join a particular group, lurk for a while and see what the group talks about and how they behave generally.

- Don't post a message to an ongoing thread about something completely different. If you want to go off at a tangent, start a new thread.

- Quote the relevant portions of a previous message if you're adding to an ongoing thread. But don't quote the whole message, or the whole previous thread.

- Don't send advertising or junk mail. However, it's OK to include references to your homepage in your sig file.

- Most discussion groups are public forums, so you should remove the personal information from your sig file. This is especially important if your children are posting to public forums on the web.

- Don't post private email to a group without permission. Re-posting material that has appeared in a group already is fine – it's deemed to be in the public domain.

- Posting a message to a public discussion space online is equivalent to publishing it. So don't post illegal or libellous material.

- Remember that there are people on the other side of the screen, so try to be constructive. People do sometimes spout the most incredible rubbish. But you can point this out without insulting them – sometimes.

- Before you start an argument, think about the rest of the group. It can be fun to watch two people slugging it out. But mostly it's a bore.

- Think a bit before you type, especially with mailing lists. Sending to a message to the whole list that was intended for one person only is easily done, and can have very embarrassing consequences.

Lurk Net slang meaning to hang around in discussion groups (and chatrooms) reading what other people have to say, but not actually saying anything yourself.

Web discussion boards

All sorts of websites – from webzines to online auctions – now feature discussion boards. There are also plenty of sites that specialize in hosting discussion groups. At Smart Groups **http://www.smartgroups.com** and Yahoo! Groups **http://groups.yahoo.com/** you can click your way through a variety of publicly accessible discussion boards or set up your own private board, an online meeting place for your real world club, business or family. Web discussion boards are very easy to use:

- When you access one, you'll usually see a list of messages.

- Some messages will have a number in brackets next to them. This indicates the number of responses that particular message has generated.

- If you click on the message, it will come up on the screen, and you'll see links to the responses it's generated.

- At the end of a message, you'll see a form you use to post a reply or send a new message. You just need to enter your email address and a subject line, then your thoughts, then press *SEND*.

Web discussion spaces' user-friendliness means that they can end up feeling less intimate and involving than other groups. Often, they're places where people can talk back to the media. And you can read some very stimulating stuff. But in general, they don't build up a group of regular users or a sense of group identity. As a result they can feel less satisfying than other online group discussions.

Online clubs Some sites now let you set up online meeting places that combine various forms of internet communication/collaboration. Yahoo! Clubs lets you set up an online group hang-out, where you can set up discussion boards and live chats, create a shared calendar and an online photo album and more. Lots of kids enjoy creating these online clubs for their friends or family. Find out more at **http://uk.clubs.yahoo.com/**.

Mailing lists

There are two types of mailing lists online.

- **One-way lists** – with these you subscribe and everything from fanzines to product information is sent to you on a regular basis.

- **Two-way lists** – here the content of the list is generated by the subscribers. Some can be pretty serious affairs. Others are more relaxed and the ostensible subject – a local pop group, gardening, whatever – takes a back seat to general chatter. Some two-way lists are controlled by a moderator who keeps discussions on track, and weeds out insulting or off-topic postings. Others are completely open. Everything anyone sends to the list goes out to everyone else, which can lead to huge amounts of mail.

A few years back, mailing lists were run using one of two software programs, Listserv or Majordomo. Once you subscribed to this kind of list, the day's messages were sent to your mailbox. Sometimes, they were archived later on a web site. In the last few years, mailing lists have moved on to the web. Topica **http://www.topica.com** hosts thousands of mailing lists and offers a little more flexibility than the old-style lists. You can choose to have a list sent to your mailbox or you can read it on the web, discussion board-style. You can also decide whether to get a digest sent to you, rather every message. It's easier to search the list's archive and research other lists too.

If you're looking for a list to subscribe to, try searching on Topica. Alternatively, if you want to try an old-style list, try Publicly Accessible Mailing Lists **http://paml.net/**. Subscribing to the lists maintained on Topica is easy. You'll find lots of information on the site. Subscribing to lists maintained using Listserv or Majordomo is slightly trickier. The general information about a list at a site like PAML will tell you what to do.

1 First, you send mail – usually with 'subscribe' in the body of the message – to the computer where the list is based.

2 You will then receive mail telling you you're on the list.

3 Save this message. It will contain details about how to post to the list and how to cancel your subscription.

4 One thing to look out for: these old-style lists have two addresses – one to which you send messages for the list proper and one for administrative queries. Don't get the two mixed up.

Whichever list you choose, joining is pretty easy. Dealing with the number of messages it can generate might prove problematic.

• If you're going on holiday, sign off from high-volume lists before you go. Don't stay on the list and use a service that automatically sends people a note saying you're on holiday: if you're on a high-volume list, you will end up replying to every message – and you may make the list unworkable.

• If you're on a high-volume list that's interesting but overwhelming, ask the administrator if there's a weekly digest of the list you can get instead.

• To avoid messages from a high-volume list clogging up your Inbox, use a mail filter to divert it to its own box. Set the filter to look for the list address or the list name, which is usually in the *SUBJECT* line of messages.

Setting up your own list If you want to start your own list, it's easily done at Topica. If you fancy running an old-style list, you'll find information about Listserv at **http://www.lsoft.com**, along with a Listserv list search engine too. You can find out more about Majordomo from **http://www.greatcircle.com/majordomo/**.

Usenet newsgroups

Usenet newsgroups are similar to mailing lists. You post messages to a group. Other members of the group post responses, and over time a kind of conversation, or thread, builds up. However, newsgroups work in a slightly different way to mailing lists. Your ISP keeps a database of newsgroup postings on its news server, a computer running the Usenet news transfer protocol. Your ISP's news server is connected to others and a steady flow of postings to the newsgroups is passed between them. You connect to the news server to access the various groups and read the latest postings. When you send a post to a particular group, it goes to your ISP's news server and is then passed on to others. Consequently, it can sometimes take a while before everyone on Usenet gets to see your witty deconstruction of David Beckham's latest haircut. If they don't access Usenet on a regular basis, they may miss it altogether.

There are thousands of newsgroups on Usenet, covering just about anything you might want to talk or argue about.

- Most are standard discussion groups, in which everyone can contribute.

- Some are one-way affairs, for announcements only.

- Others are primarily for exchanging files (anything from images to software).

- A few are strictly moderated – with moderators filtering all the messages that go the group and only allowing through those that fit various criteria.

- Most newsgroups aren't moderated. However, as you'll discover, that doesn't mean they don't have rules about who can say what.

Usenet newsgroups are probably the most demanding of the various online discussion forums. Usenet in general is one of the more controversial areas of the net, mainly because a large chunk of it is driven by uncensored human desire. As mentioned above, there's a lot of illegal/adult material in the newsgroups. They're definitely not for younger kids. I think you should give them a look, if only so that you can decide whether you want your teenage kids to use them. Techno-gurus say the net is a new public realm where everyone can have their say. Usenet is one of the things that lives up to the rhetoric... sort of. It shows you the consequences of that rhetoric. If you want to see what a people-driven info-anarchy actually looks like, visit the newsgroups. They can be both heart-warming and kind of scary. They aren't always pretty, but they are often interesting.

Choosing a newsreader

To access the newsgroups, you need a newsreader. Both Microsoft's email package Outlook Express and Netscape 6 Mail are also newsreaders. If you're just starting out, they'll be fine. Alternatively, PC owners could try Free Agent **http://www.forteinc.com/getfa/getfa.htm**. Mac users could try Newswatcher **http://charlotte.at.northwestern.edu/jln/progs.ssi**. For more newsreaders, try **http://www.newsreaders.com/**.

To access your browser's newsreader:

- In Outlook Express:
  1 Look for the READ NEWS link on the introductory screen once you've launched the main program.

2 Alternatively, click on your news server's name in the *FOLDERS* window on the left

- In Netscape 6:

  1 Select the *TASKS* menu, then *MAIL*.

Configuring your newsreader

You need to enter details about yourself and the address of your ISP's news server – the computer that maintains a database of newsgroups. Your news server address is usually something like **news.yourisp.net**.

- In Internet Explorer:

  1 Select the *TOOLS* menu, then *INTERNET ACCOUNTS*. Then click the *NEWS* tab.

  2 To add a new news account, use the *ADD* button, then *NEWS*. The *INTERNET CONNECTION WIZARD* will start up and take you through the configuration process.

  3 To change an old one, click the *PROPERTIES* button and follow the directions.

- In Netscape Mail:

  1 Select the *EDIT* menu, then *MAIL / NEWS ACCOUNT SETTINGS*. Then click the *NEW ACCOUNT* button.

  2 An *ACCOUNT WIZARD* will then take you through configuration.

- In the Mac version of Outlook Express:

  1 Select the *TOOLS* menu, then *ACCOUNTS*, then *NEWS*.

  2 Click on the account you want, then *EDIT* to change any details.

  3 Click on *NEW* to add a new server.

Getting started

The first time you start your newsreader, it should automatically download a complete list of newsgroups from your ISP's news server. Groups are arranged in hierarchies – fairly wide-ranging thematic categories – followed by more specific detail about what the group discusses. For example, **uk.politics.censorship** would, as you might expect, be devoted to discussing the politics of censorship in the UK only. There are plenty of hierarchies – some easy to decipher, others rather mystifying. Here are a few of the more popular ones:

alt	As in alternative – discussions with a non-conformist / anarchic / funky flavour
biz	You can send your commercial messages here
comp	Discussions about everything to do with computers
microsoft	Get your product support advice here
misc	Catch-all category for stuff that doesn't seem to fit in elsewhere
news	Home to announcements about Usenet and debates on what's wrong with it
rec	Recreation, as in sports, hobbies and the like
sci	Science
soc	For socio-cultural discussion (and a bit of religion as well)
talk	The place to argue out more controversial issues – gun control, for example
uk	Devoted to UK-specific discussions.

When it comes to finding a newsgroup, you could browse the general list. Alternatively, most newsreaders let you search the list. To subscribe to a group:

- **In Outlook Express:**
  1 Select the *TOOLS* menu, then *NEWSGROUPS*.
  2 A *NEWSGROUPS SUBSCRIPTIONS* dialog box will come up. There's a search box at the top, and you can search via simple key words – comics, "The Simpsons", shopping.
  3 Once you find a group you like, click on it, then click on the *SUBSCRIBE* button.

- **In Netscape Mail 6:**
  1 Select the *FILE* menu, then *SUBSCRIBE*. A *SUBSCRIBE* dialog box will come up.
  2 Browse the list for something you're interested in.
  3 Once you find a group you like, click on it, then click on the *SUBSCRIBE* button.

- **In the Mac version of Outlook Express:**
  1 Click on the name of your news server in the left-hand window. The newsgroup list will come up in the main window with a search box above it.
  2 Highlight a group and click the *SUBSCRIBE* toolbar button.

Your ISP might not provide access to all the available news-groups. ISPs often don't carry specialist or foreign-language groups. If you want access to those groups, ask them. They will usually oblige. ISPs also don't carry groups that might contain illegal material (i.e. child porn or pirated software). Some ISPs and online services specifically target the family market and as a result block whole chunks of Usenet, for example, all of the alt.sex. With the net, there's often a way round censorship. If

ISPs block certain newsgroups, users can find them via publicly accessible news servers. There's more about this on Newzbot **http://www.newzbot.com** – watch out for computer-literate teens using this to get round attempts to stop them using the newsgroups.

Reading newsgroups

Once you've subscribed to a few groups, you need to download the most recent messages. Once you're connected:

- In Outlook Express:

  1 There will be a list of groups you've subscribed to in the window on the left of the screen. Connect to your ISP then click on one of these groups.

  2 Outlook Express will download the headers from the newest messages. Click on a header and the whole message will be downloaded.

  3 Outlook Express is set to download 300 headers by default, usually enough to get a feel for most groups. You can change this to a higher or lower figure.

  4 Select the *TOOLS* menu, then *OPTIONS*, then click the *READ* tab and change the line *DOWNLOAD 300 HEADERS AT A TIME*.

  5 In the Mac version, to find a similar section, select the *TOOLS* menu, then *ACCOUNTS*, then *NEWS*, highlight the relevant account, then click on *EDIT*, then *OPTIONS*.

- **In Netscape Mail 6:**

  1 To the left of the window, under your news server's name, there should be a list of the news groups you've subscribed to. Double-click the one you want to read.

  2 Netscape 6 will now download the headers from the newest messages. It's set by default to ask before it downloads more than 500 message headers. To change this, select the *EDIT* menu, then *MAIL / NEWS ACCOUNT SETTINGS*. Look for your newsgroup account in the box on the left of the *ACCOUNT SETTINGS* dialog box. Click on *SERVER SETTINGS* under it. Remove the tick next to *ASK ME BEFORE DOWNLOADING MORE THAN 500 MESSAGES*.

  3 Once you've downloaded the number of headers you want, a window will open, showing the headers in the top part of the screen.

  4 Click on a message on the list and its contents will appear in the bottom part of the window.

Headers In this context, headers are the basic details about the message: what it's about, who sent it and when. They are not the message itself. You'll need to go back online to get that.

The most sensible way to consume Usenet is offline. Once you've subscribed to a few groups, you should get the latest messages, log off and then read them.

- **In Outlook Express:**

  1 Download the headers from your newsgroup, then log off. Set Outlook Express to work offline, via the *FILE* menu.

  2 In the main window, you'll see a list of headers, some with a + sign next to them. Click on this and you'll see the thread (i.e. the various replies) this particular message has generated.

3 Next you need to mark the postings you're interested in. To the left of the headers, click in the column underneath the arrow pointing downward. A little blue arrow will appear to the left of the header.

4 Once you've marked the messages, select the *TOOLS* menu, then *MARK FOR OFFLINE*, then *DOWNLOAD MESSAGE LATER*.

5 Go online, select the *TOOLS* menu, and then *SYNCHRONIZE NEWSGROUP*. Outlook Express will then connect and download the stuff you want.

- **In Netscape Mail 6:**

  1 Download the headers you want, then log off.

  2 Select the newsgroup you're interested in, so that the headers are displayed in the main window.

  3 Mark the messages you want. There are several ways you can do this: the easiest is probably to hold down the *CONTROL* key, then click on each of the messages you want.

  4 Once that's done, select the *FILE* menu, then *OFFLINE*, then *GET SELECTED MESSAGES*. Your newsreader will connect and download the messages. Then you can log off and start reading.

  5 Alternatively, you can download the new messages from a whole group for reading offline by selecting *FILE*, then *OFFLINE*, then *DOWNLOAD / SYNC MESSAGES*. Click the *SELECT* button in the dialog box that pops up and then you can pick the groups you want to view offline. Then put a tick next to *NEWSGROUP MESSAGES* and *WORK OFFLINE ONCE DOWNLOAD AND/OR SYNC IS COMPLETED*. Then click *OK*.

Actually, both newsreaders offer several ways of reading messages offline. It might be worth trying each out to see which you like best. For more information, try the help files.

Reading the newsgroups

It can take a while to get into some newsgroups. Stick with a group over a few days and it should start to make sense. After a while you may realize that some group members are complete time-wasters. You can get your newsreader to block their messages. This is one area in which stand-alone newsreaders have the edge, though Outlook Express isn't bad.

- In Outlook Express:

  1 Highlight a post by the offending individual, then select the *MESSAGE* menu, then *BLOCK SENDER*.

  2 Alternatively, to create more versatile filters, select the *TOOLS* menu, then *MESSAGE RULES*, then *NEWS*. You can then choose to delete messages from certain people or messages that have certain words in the title.

- In the Mac version of Outlook Express:

  1 Block certain messages by selecting the *TOOLS* menu, then *RULES*, then *NEWS*, then *NEW*.

  2 You can then specify the criteria for blocking messages.

Posting messages

If you do something wrong in a newsgroup, or just ask a silly question, you will be flamed by someone. So before you send in a message, do some research. That way you won't present too big a target.

- Read the newsgroup for a while – see how the group works, who contributes the most, what the group likes and doesn't like.

- Each group has a file of Frequently Asked Questions (FAQ) detailing what the group discusses and how. Read it – you should find it at the Internet FAQ Archives **http://faqs.org/**. That way, you should be able to avoid sending messages/questions which people will dismiss as obvious/already dealt with.

- You can find a lengthy guide to newsgroup netiquette, some amusing parodies and useful information on the UK Usenet homepages **http://www.usenet.org.uk**.

OK, so you've read a message you want to reply to:

- **In Outlook Express:**
  1 Click either the *REPLY TO GROUP* button (to send your thoughts to the group) or the *REPLY TO SENDER* button (to send your message to the author of the post you're responding to – it's considered good netiquette to do this).
  2 You can do both at the same time by selecting the *MESSAGE* menu, then *REPLY TO ALL*.
  3 Whatever you choose, a new window opens, with the address filled out and the previous message quoted. Edit it and add your response.
  4 Then click the *SEND* button on the toolbar.

- **In Netscape Mail 6:**
  1 Click either the *REPLY* button (to send the message to the newsgroup) or the *REPLY ALL BUTTON*. This simultaneously sends messages to the newsgroup and the original author of the post.
  2 A new window will open, with the address filled out and the previous message quoted. Edit it and add your response.
  3 Then click the *SEND* button on the toolbar.

Messages to newsgroups are often cross-posted, i.e. they're sent to several groups that share some interest in a general subject. When you reply to a cross-posting, your message will be sent to all the groups the previous message was cross-posted to. You'll see them entered in the address field.

To post an original message:

- **In Outlook Express:**
  1. In the window on the left side of the screen, where your subscriptions list is, click on the group you want to post to. Then click the *NEW POST* button on the toolbar.
  2. Write something suitably pithy in the *SUBJECT* line, then write your thoughts in the text box at the bottom.
  3. When you're done, click the *SEND* button.

- **In Netscape Mail 6:**
  1. Select the group you want to post to from the list on the left side of the browser window and then click the *NEW MSG* button.
  2. Write something in the *SUBJECT* line, then write your thoughts in the text box.
  3. Click *SEND* when you're done.

There are a few things you should look out for when sending an original message:

- Don't cross-post it to groups you don't know. It's a good way to annoy people. Remember – they have your email address and they will let you know how they feel.

- You may be tempted to try sending a test message to check you've got all this right. But don't send a test post to a regular newsgroup, which is another sure-fire way to upset people.

- Some ISPs have their own test newsgroups and there's also an alt.test group you can try instead.

- If you have a question on the subject covered by the newsgroup, tell people to answer with private email to you when you post it, then post a summary of responses to the group. That way, the group won't get clogged with people sending the same answer.

- Don't assume that newsgroup users are just dying to help out with students' homework/dissertations. Don't send a questionnaire on a particular subject to a newsgroup. It annoys people – understandably – and you won't get any useful replies.

- Instead, hang out in relevant newsgroups, identify the more knowledgeable members and send them private email asking if they have time to answer a few questions. Then send your questionnaire.

- If you're looking for answers, your best bet may be to tap the archived collective wisdom of Usenet via the Deja archives, which now reside on Google at **http://groups.google.com/**.

With Outlook Express, if you do send a message to a group by mistake, you can retrieve the situation by sending a cancel message. This will remove the posting (although it takes time and if someone downloads the message before your cancel message reaches the group, there's nothing you can do).

- **In Outlook Express:**
  1 Highlight the message you posted.
  2 Select the *MESSAGE* menu, then *CANCEL MESSAGE*.

Newsgroups and attachments

In the past, dealing with files attached to Usenet postings could be tricky, but the latest newsreaders make the whole thing easy. They work in exactly the same way as email attachments – go to page 117 for general advice. UUencode was the standard way to convert attachments on Usenet. It's been replaced by MIME. Outlook Express and Netscape 6 Mail can handle both, but if you're using an older newsreader you may have problems. A group FAQ might have advice on how to convert attachments posted to the group. Alternatively, hang out in the group to see what everyone else does.

Newsgroups and HTML postings

When you're composing a reply or a new message to a newsgroup, you can format it in HTML – in other words you can send messages with links, graphics and embedded images. However, before you send your flashy message, find out whether it's appropriate. Many groups prefer plain text. See what seems to be acceptable in the group in question. For information on how to change the format of your newsgroup postings from HTML to text or vice versa, go to page 118 in the email section.

Online chat

If you're not actually talking/typing yourself, online chat can look a bit silly. Sure the idea sounds good – people from all around the world having a conversation that scrolls out in real-time text across their computer screens. But often the reality is a disjointed ream of gibberish that ends up going nowhere in particular. The thing to remember here is that the net is not a spectator sport. Online chat is very dull to watch. But do it yourself and, even if you're only exchanging banalities, it can be exciting.

How chat can benefit your family:

- Chat isn't really for young children. They won't be able to type fast enough to enjoy it. However, they might enjoy a session in which you help them chat to far-flung relatives.

- Many teenagers love chat. For them it's a great new way to do what teens have always loved to do – hang out with their mates and shoot the breeze.

- Chat can be a great way for families to stay in touch. Many families who live far apart now set up private chatrooms where they can sort out important business or just catch up with the latest news.

- Online services like AOL and big websites like Yahoo! host special events in their chat spaces where kids can talk/type to celebrities and ask them questions.

Potential problems with email that parents need to be aware of:

- Some teenagers find chat very compelling and will spend hours in their favourite chatrooms.

- Much chat does revolve around sex. In fact, to a lot of people it is a form of sex in itself. People meet online, then head off to private rooms to type dirty to each other. Much of this takes place in adult chat spaces. That said, many teenagers flirt and more in the chat-rooms set aside for them on websites and online services.

- Women are often verbally abused and even harassed in chat-rooms. The solution is for women (and children) is to pick non-gender specific screen names or use their chat software to block persistent idiots.

- In general, people aren't often what they seem in chatrooms. People embellish – they make out they're better looking/cooler/richer than they are in real life. Many of those who say they're women are men indulging in a bit of online cross-dressing. The real problem, though, is adults pretending to be kids. There is plenty of evidence that paedophiles frequent chatrooms and try to engage children in conversation. Their aim is to build relationships, get kids to trust them and ultimately meet them offline.

- Arguments can blow up very quickly in chatrooms – much as they do in discussion groups. And these arguments can lead to other problems – harassment, threats and more.

- Many chatrooms are really only for adults. In particular, the Internet Relay Chat network isn't for children. Older teenagers might enjoy it, but be aware that the chatrooms there aren't really moderated. In addition some IRC chatrooms are home to people who exchange illegal material – pirated software and music, for example. Others are home to hackers who might indulge in mischief at your expense if you let them.

So parents need to take care when it comes to their children chatting online. You can use technology to deal with some of the problems posed by chat. But you also need to talk to your kids about chat. You need to set guidelines, teach them not to give out personal information and offer advice on problems to look out for or avoid. You should also make sure that your kids use only chat spaces supervised by a grown-up human (many chatrooms are actually patrolled by bots – automated programs that scan for people breaking the rules, usually using bad language. These are all right but they're not as good as a real person when it comes to keeping order and making sure dubious people are kept out. Chat has a bad reputation. But you shouldn't get too hung up over the potential problems. If you're sensible, your kids will enjoy it. There's more advice on all this on page 245.

....

Places to chat online: online services

....

Chat has always been important to online services like AOL. In fact, it paid their bills in the early days. AOL in particular still hosts thousands of rooms, devoted to all sorts of subjects. Chat in the online services is a pretty organized thing, with regular events in which users can get advice from experts and put questions to celebrities and politicians. It's also subject to some control – in theory. If someone bothers you, you can report them to a moderator. Though AOL likes to sell itself as a family operation, things can get pretty steamy in a lot of their adult chatrooms. However, parents who want to make sure their kids aren't exposed to dirty typing can block their access to certain rooms.

Webchat

Many websites – from the big pages maintained by ISPs and the likes of Yahoo! and Microsoft to webzines – now feature chatrooms. The basic format is the same as AOL: various rooms devoted to different topics. Again, they sometimes host special events. The main attraction of web chat is that it's happening on the web, so you can use your browser without resorting to separate software. To access many web chatrooms, you generally need an up-to-date browser – i.e. one that can run Java or Javascript. When you enter the chatroom, your browser loads a Java chat applet. However, many web chatrooms now also run in HTML too.

> **Java, Javascript, applet** Java is a programming language which, among other things, can be used to create interactive multimedia effects on the web. Javascript is a similar sort of language. An applet is a small program written in Java that can be placed on a webpage.

Internet Relay Chat (IRC)

To chat using IRC, which was created by the Finnish programmer Jarkko Oikarinen in 1988, you have to connect to a chat server. Groups of chat servers around the world are hooked up into networks, known as nets. Much like an online service, a particular net will host a bewildering amount of chat spaces (known as channels), each in theory devoted to a particular subject. Though not as organized as AOL, IRC nets do host celebrity chats, special events and even games. In general, IRC is rather anarchic – it isn't really for kids, though some teenagers will enjoy it. Compared to the online services, it is harder to use.

Chat style and netiquette

For beginners, simply following a conversation in a chatroom can be tricky. Thanks to delays on the line (known as the lag factor on the net), everyone usually seems to be talking at once, often in weird variants of something that once resembled English. But if you persist, you can usually pick up the thread. As with discussion groups, before you contribute yourself, lurk for a while and find out how the chatroom works. In chat spaces, everyone knows you are lurking; your arrival is always announced to all the other users. So if someone does say hello, it's bad form not to respond. The basic idea with chat is to keep the conversation going and to remember that it is a conversation. Here's a few tips that might come in handy:

- Don't change the subject of an ongoing chat or start talking about something unconnected with the room's designated subject.

- If you have a lot to say, break it down into shorter chunks. Keeping things short is always the best policy with chat.

- The TLAs and smileys people use in their mail can be useful in real-time chat. Once you get used to them, the former can speed up your typing – it still won't be anything like normal spoken conversation, but it helps. The latter can help resolve misunderstandings caused by bad typing or delays on the line.

- Capitals are the equivalent of shouting and should be avoided.

- Watch your language. Chatrooms are supposed to be free and easy but many have rules about the kind of language that is permissible. If you break them, you'll be booted off. Incidentally, some chatrooms and chat programs let you block bad language.

- Always think before you type. Don't immediately kick off a flame war in response to something that seems like an insult. It may not be intended that way.

> **Chat netiquette** For a useful, albeit specialist guide to chat / IRC netiquette, which advises you to 'consider the lag factor', avoid 'attention-seeking gimmicks' and much else, go to **http://mirc.stealth.net/misc/chanrule.html**.

Chat on the web

The web is probably the easiest place to start with online chat. The only difficult thing with web chat is finding the right place to do it. There are chat spaces all over the web these days and most work in roughly the same way. Why not start with Yahoo! Chat UK **http://uk.chat.yahoo.com/** ?

1 You'll need to register first. Before you do, you'll have to read their extended terms of service and code of conduct. Once you've accepted this, you go on to registration proper.

2 There you can choose your screen name, password and the rest, before going to the Chat front page.

3 You'll see links to currently featured chatrooms, along with a link to a *COMPLETE ROOM* list. You'll also see a *FAVOURITE ROOMS* list, which

lets you access certain spaces quickly, and a *FRIENDS IN CHAT* list – once you assemble this, you can see when your friends are online and go directly to chat with them.

4 Pick a room – either from the *FEATURED ROOMS* list or the *COMPLETE ROOMS* list – and click on it.

When the chat window proper loads (which may take a while), it will be packed with frames.

1 To the right of the window, you'll see a *CHATTERS* list of people in the room.

2 To the left, taking up the bulk of the window, is the chat. Yahoo! uses a colour-coding scheme to make it easier to follow. People are shown in red type, what they say is in black.

3 Below the buttons, you'll find the text box. Type your contribution in here, then hit *RETURN* to get involved.

4 You'll find buttons to colour your contribution, bold it, underline it or italicize it at the bottom left of the chat window. The *EMOTIONS* button calls up a list of emotions you can send with your chat message – things like 'cackle', 'cringe', 'snicker' and 'snivel'. Just select one from the scrolling menu, then double-click on it. It will appear on the screen next to your name.

To send a private message to someone in the room:

1 Click on their name in the *CHATTERS* list, then on the *PM* button below the list.

2 Then fill out the pop-up box that appears.

If you want to send an emotion to another user:

1 Click on the *EMOTIONS* button, then select an emotion from the list.

2 Highlight the user's name in the *CHATTERS* box, and then press *EMOTE USER* at the bottom of the *EMOTIONS* box.

To see if any of the friends on your list is currently chatting somewhere on Yahoo!:

1   Click the *FRIENDS* button below the main chat window.

Below the main chat frame, in the bottom left-hand corner, is a general navigation menu. The buttons are generally pretty easy to understand:

- Clicking on *WHO'S CHATTING* calls up a vast list of everyone currently on Yahoo!, along with the chatroom they're chatting in and some information from their personal profiles.

- Click on *CREATE A ROOM* and a menu comes up that lets you choose a name for your chatroom, specify whether it is public or private, and so on.

If you create a public user room, it appears on the general *ROOMS* list. A private room won't. The only way people can enter it is if you invite them. To do that:

1   Click on the *MORE* button under the *CHATTERS* List.

2   Type in the name of the person you want to invite and click the *INVITE* button.

3   Alternatively, you can invite other chatters to your room through the *WHO'S CHATTING* list.

4   Locate a name in the list and click the *INVITE* link.

Web chatrooms don't seem to draw crowds of regulars or build up a real sense of community. They often seem to be populated by people there on a whim. As a result, they can be chaotic. Since they are so easy to access, people do drop in just to shout rude words or wind people up. There are things you can do:

1   To ignore them, click on their name in the *CHATTERS* box, then press the *IGNORE* button.

2 If someone is hassling you with private messages, click the
   PREFERENCES button and uncheck *POP UP NEW PRIVATE MESSAGES*.
   Now, when other chatters try to send you a private message, it should
   appear instead on the main chat screen with (PRIVATE) before the
   message and a *REPLY* link after it.

There are lots of other things you can do in Yahoo!'s chatrooms. For more tips, try the Help section
http://help.yahoo.com/help/uk/chat/.

....

IRC and kids
....

Teenage kids who love to chat may want to progress to using
IRC. Obviously, it's your decision whether you let them. If you
do let them use IRC, talk to them a bit about what they want to
do there, the problems they might encounter and the precautions they should take. To access IRC, they'll need special
software. PC owners should go for mIRC **http://www.mirc.co.uk**;
Mac users should try IRCLE **http://www.ircle.com/**. Whatever
chat software they use, they'll need to take some care setting it
up. You might want to help them out.

First, you'll probably need to specify an IRC server to
connect to. As mentioned before, chat servers are hooked up
in nets. Whatever chat server you connect to, you'll be
able to access the channels being hosted on the net that it's
a part of. There are all sorts of different nets, each with
their own distinctive flavour – for more information, go to
http://www.irchelp.org/irchelp/networks/. In the meantime, here's
a few you could try:

Undernet – **http://www.undernet.org/**

Dalnet – **http://www.dal.net/**

KidLink (an IRC net for kids) – **http://www.kidlink.org/rti/irc/index.cfm**

When you're just starting out, don't worry too much about which net to use. Chat programs like mIRC have lists of chat servers/nets you can use.

1   Pick one reasonably close to home.

2   Next you need to enter your name, email address and nickname. As mentioned before, women in particular might want to enter a fake name. There are various computer commands which let IRC users look at the information you enter – they might discover that you are actually a woman, for example.

3   If your email address reveals your real name, enter a fake one instead.

4   Nicknames are fairly straightforward. If your kids pick something provocative, they'll draw the wrong kind of attention. In addition, some names won't be acceptable in some IRC channels.

5   Some chat programs let you take measures to retain a degree of privacy on IRC – you can set things up so that people won't be able to find you online unless they know your exact nickname. Look in the *HELP* files for tips.

Once you're ready to chat:

1   Click the *CONNECT* button (or something similar). You'll then connect with the server you chose when you configured your software.

2   A screen should come up with general information – a message of the day and some details about the person responsible for the server.

3   A list of the channels available on this particular net should then open automatically. If it doesn't, you can usually call it up via a toolbar button.

4   To join a channel, just click the *JOIN* button. When you're just starting out, look for channels like #newbies, #newusers, #beginners or #ircbeginners. (Note that all IRC channels start with the # sign.)

Once you've joined a channel:

1 You should see a listing of the people currently on the channel.

2 Below the main chat window, you'll see the text box where you enter your contributions. When you first arrive, it's polite to say hello to everyone. Type 'Hello' in the text box then hit *RETURN*.

3 After that, lurk for a while and see what's happening.

4 If this channel really isn't you, you can leave by just closing the window.

IRC and text commands

Most new IRC programs feature plenty of user-friendly toolbar buttons. But you can also use text commands to get things done. You type the command then press *RETURN*. Anything preceded by / is interpreted by chat programs as a command. Always remember the / sign. If you miss it out, your software will assume you've typed some chat and will broadcast it to the channel. Here's a few commands you might find useful:

• You can join a channel by typing /join #newbies in the main text box, then hitting *RETURN*.

• You can leave a channel by typing /part.

• If you want to find out whether a friend is chatting on the system, type /whois, then their nickname.

There are loads more things you can do – from sending coloured text to creating a new channel. Look in the mIRC help files for a list of commands you can use. Alternatively, you'll find lots of advice at IRC Help **http://www.irchelp.org**, the mIRC homepage – **http://www.mirc.co.uk/** and New IRC Users **http://www.newircusers.com/**.

IRC and safety

Some IRC users seem to like nothing better than trying to take over certain chat channels. You aren't likely to run into the more malevolent kind of IRC user unless you go looking for them. However, there are precautions you can take:

- If someone asks you to type a particular computer command, don't ever do it, whatever they say. It will probably do something nasty to your PC and may even let someone else control it. Similarly, don't click on a file that someone you don't know sends to you, whatever they say it is.

- Remember that you don't have to accept private messages. If someone hassles you via private messages, raise the problem in the public part of the channel or get help from the person in charge of the channel (known as the op).

- Alternatively, type /motd to get the Message of the Day, which should feature contact details for the system administrator.

- You can set your software to ignore certain users. Type /ignore then the nickname of the user.

- IRC software, mIRC in particular, allows you to be much more specific when it comes to ignoring people and messages, so look in its help files.

Graphic chat

Chat isn't just a text thing. There are places online where people can represent themselves on screen as characters in 2D or 3D space – their speech appears in comic-strip style bubbles. Microsoft Chat was one of the first programs to offer this kind of thing. Now you can find it in lots of places on the web. Older teenagers might enjoy:

- Dobedo **http://www.dobedo.co.uk**. Once you've signed up, you can design yourself a cartoony avatar (your visual representation on the net). When people are chatting with you, they'll see that image in a particular space.

- Cycosmos **http://www.cycosmos.co.uk**. Here the avatars you design have a more realistic look. You can also specify a personality for your online self. You can then search for other users with particular character types and chat with them or mail them.

MUDS

MUDs (Multi-User Dimensions or Dungeons) are text-based role-playing games that take place online, which makes them sound rather dull. Their fans might prefer to see them as alternative worlds spun out of text, where users can play out ideas, theories and fantasies. MUDs started out as online extensions of Dungeons and Dragons-style role-playing games. People competed to become wizards and kings. But then some MUDs dropped the gaming side and became more sociable, like digital communes where people explored alternative identities and lifestyles. MUDs aren't for kids. Some would argue they're not really for grown-ups either. Perhaps the best thing to say is that they attract adolescents of all ages. They're not quite as popular as they used to be, but some teenagers can get very caught up in them nevertheless. They may just be text. But the combination of real-time chat with a kind of ongoing fantasy world which lets them construct different selves in collaboration with others can end up being much more compelling than the latest 3-D game. If your teenage child gets interested in MUDs, it's worth making sure they don't get too stuck on them. For an introduction to MUDs, try the MUD FAQ at **http://www.lysator.liu.se/mud/faq/faq1.html**. Some computer games companies are attempting to introduce graphic MUDs, in which you can see the world you're playing in. Ultima Online **http://www.uo.com** was the first graphic MUD-style game – it provided an online extension to an existing computer game. Many fans now prefer Sony's Everquest **http://www.station.sony.com/everquest/**.

Instant messages

When instant message programs first appeared, they were a bit like intelligent online pagers. They told you when friends came online and let you message them to say hello and chat a little. Now IM programs are all-purpose communications tools, and instant messaging is probably the most popular online activity, especially with teenagers, who send lots more IMs than email. How come? IM programs make that essential modern teenage pursuit – hanging out with friends online and talking about nothing – that much easier. In addition, you also need to create a list of your friends for your IM software to work – something that seems to appeal to the teenage mind. What better way to show that someone is definitely out than removing them from your IM buddy list?

How instant messaging can benefit your family:

• IM programs tell your teenage children as soon as their friends log on and let them get in touch and chat straight away.

- They let them set up chat sessions while they're doing other things online. They don't have to visit a specific chatroom and look for their friends.

- Working parents who want to chat to their kids when they come home from school will find an IM program useful. It will tell you as soon as they log on.

- An IM program will also let you keep an eye on them. If you've said the net is off-limits until their homework is done, you'll know when they're breaking your rules.

Potential problems with instant messaging parents need to be aware of:

- Some children do find it very compelling and will do little else if you let them.

- Instant message programs tell people when you come online and will make other information about you available unless you take action. You can see how this could be abused. However, with the best programs, you can stop people adding your number without your authorization. You can also block messages from certain users.

The most popular instant message program is ICQ **http:// www.icq.com** (as in 'I seek you'). Aside from letting you send text to your friends, you can use it to:

- Send voice messages via the net or send text messages to mobile phones.

- Surf the web with friends and swap ideas about the sites you see.

- Access different content channels and get news headlines and sports results.

- Swap files and play online games.

ICQ's rivals include:

Microsoft Messenger http://messenger.msn.com

Yahoo! Messenger http://pager.yahoo.com/

AOL Instant Messenger http://www.aol.co.uk/aim/

Jabber http://www.hotjabber.com/

The next most popular of these after ICQ is AOL Instant Messenger, which will let you message AOL users, anyone else who has registered the software, and ICQ users. It's bundled with Netscape 6, so you'll probably already have a copy. In fact, AOL Instant Messenger is integrated with the main browser, so that you can access your buddy list via *MY SIDEBAR*. Obviously with messaging systems, the number of users you can reach is one of the key things to look for. ICQ and AIM are the two leading programs and they can talk to each other, so they're the ones to go for.

AOL Instant Messenger has lots of useful features, aside from basic messaging:

- You can send friends images and voice messages.

- You can specify who can contact you and also block messages from certain users.

- There's also a *WARN* feature that sends a warning to abusive users (and the AOL authorities).

But if instant messaging is your thing, you'll probably want to use ICQ:

- It has more features – everything from sending files to browsing the web with friends.

- It does the basic paging job really well. For example, if you instant message someone and they're offline, it holds on to your message and sends it when they come online.

- It also has reasonable privacy controls – your authorization is required before people can add you to their buddy list, and you can block messages from certain users.

You can download ICQ from **http://www.icq.com**.

1 Once you install it, you need to register and get a password and a screen number.

2 You pass the screen number on to friends who want to message you. You use their numbers to create a 'buddy list' of friends who also use the same software, so that when they come online you're notified, via a small window on your desktop (obviously you have to be online too).

3 You can then chat if you want or an awful lot more besides.

The best place to find out more is the ICQ site, where you'll find lengthy guides to the software and what you can do with it. For more news and lots of tips, try C Net's ICQ section **http://www.cnet.com/internet/0-3782.html**.

The next level

Net shopping

Some people see the whole dot.com crash as proof that shopping online was always a silly idea and was bound to fail. They're wrong. There may be fewer net shops in business now than there were a couple of years ago. But more of us are now actually buying things online. Of course, much of the hype that surrounded net shopping at the end of the nineties was ludicrous. It's not about to completely replace real-world shops – most of us enjoy visiting our favourite real-world stores, whether they're bookshops or high fashion boutiques. We're not going to give that up. On the other hand, it is possible to overstate the sensual pleasures of the weekly supermarket shop. It's true that there are lots of products that aren't really suited to net shopping. You probably wouldn't want to buy a designer suit online. But books, CDs, videos, video games and computer software are different. They're portable and you don't need to touch them to know roughly what you're getting. The same goes for travel and financial services. Buying computer hardware and electronic gadgets online is becoming more popular, as is online supermarket shopping.

How shopping on the net can benefit your family:

- All parents know about the value of mail order. In a way, net shopping is mail order with interactive knobs on. It's easy and convenient. Without leaving home, you can have access to a wider range of products than you can find on your local high street.

- You will save time if you buy online. You may also save money. The prices aren't quite as low as during the dot.com boom, but there are still bargains online.

- Net shops offer lots of interesting services. Based on what you've already bought, some recommend other products they think you'll like. Most will gift-wrap presents for you. Some let you put up a wish list of things you want – this can work quite well for older, teenage kids who want to give their relatives some clues about presents.

- The net lets you shop abroad. If you're looking for that must-have toy, and all the real-world shops have sold out, the net might be able to help.

- The online auctions will be very useful if you or your children collect certain sorts of toys, games, comics, books or whatever. They might also come in handy if your kids get fed up with their collection and want to sell it.

Problems with net shopping that parents need to be aware of:

- Net shops like Amazon can offer various personalized services (like recommendations) because they create cookies – little identifying files on your browser that allow them to track what you do on their site and what you buy. There are privacy implications here you might want to think about – more on this on page 262.

- If you leave your credit card information lying around in an easily accessible form (e.g. in a file on your computer), your kids will be able to use it online, and you may end up having to pick up the tab for their spending sprees. Similarly, if you leave the password to an account at a net shop lying around, you may also have problems.

- Some net shops offer one-click buying services. They use the information you've previously entered (your address and credit card details) and let you buy something by just pressing one button. If you set this up on a family computer, it means your kids can buy stuff easily without knowing your credit card data. So be careful.

You need to think about security and safety in general when shopping on the net – more on this shortly.

Navigating online shops

Some of the first net shops mistakenly attempted to simulate supermarkets and shopping malls. Smarter outfits quickly saw that you didn't have to digitally mock up shelves full of beans on your website, and that the net let you experiment with new ways of selling. The most successful online retailers, however, have realized that the net shopping experience needs to be familiar as well as different. Take the leading online retailer Amazon **http://www.amazon.co.uk**. Visit their books department and you find top ten charts, reviews and interviews. You can also post reviews of books you've read. Amazon cross-references its records, so that it can recommend titles purchased by people who bought the same books as you. You can also get email updates about new titles on subjects you're interested in. But when it comes to buying something, the process is very simple. You make a list of what you want, you enter your credit card details, and the stuff gets sent to you.

Making an online purchase

This tends to work in the same way at most online shops:

1 You browse for the product you want, then press a *BUY* button, which adds the item to your online 'shopping cart'.

2 Once you're ready to pay, you press the *CHECKOUT* button.

3 You go to a page where you enter your details – name, address, credit card number.

4 You choose a shipping method.

5   The total cost is totted up and you're given an opportunity to confirm the purchase or change your mind.

6   Then it's just a question of waiting for your goods to arrive.

7   Some online retailers email you to confirm the purchase and will also send an update on your order's progress. Alternatively, many sites let you check the progress of your orders on their sites, via an area devoted to your account.

8   Once you've entered your personal/credit card information, most net shops will store it securely, so that you don't have to enter it again when you want to buy something else. All you'll have to do to access your account data is to enter your password and email address.

> **Check the delivery costs**   Once you start browsing round online shops, you may be surprised by some of the prices. You'll often find 20% off the standard prices for books, CDs and videos. But before you buy, check the delivery charges (and times). These can add up. You can still come out ahead, compared to the high street. But it pays to check.

Safe shopping

The panic about giving out your credit card details while shopping online probably has more to do with novelty than with real risks. Giving your credit card number to someone over the telephone is potentially problematic, but most of us do it without thinking. There are various things you can do to make sure your credit card information remains safe:

• Make sure that personal information and credit card details are sent to a secure server. Both Navigator and Internet Explorer are set up for secure transactions (they use something called Secure

Sockets Layer (SSL) technology to make sure that important information is encrypted when it is sent over the net).

- If you're connected to a secure server, you should see a little graphic of a locked padlock at the bottom of your browser screen. Some earlier browsers use the image of a key. If it's broken, you aren't on a secure site.

- You can also check by looking at the address in the browser location bar. If you're on a secure server, the URL should start with **https://**.

- When you enter a secure site, your browser may also flash a dialog box telling you as much (you'll see another one when you leave).

Incidentally, if you use a credit card, you are protected in various ways against fraud online. Some net shops also offer protection (money-back guarantees and the like), if you can prove that you were the victim of online fraud. And if you're worried about sending details over the net, a good online retailer should give you the option of telephoning them in. Secure servers do offer the consumer pretty good protection. To stay safe, there are other things you can do:

- Don't ever shop on a site that isn't secure.

- Don't send your personal information and credit card details by ordinary email.

- Don't give out any more information than you would with a standard credit-card purchase via the telephone.

- Before you buy anything, check out the retailer. Make sure they have a real-world address and telephone number. Don't buy from a company with just an email address. Check the refund and return policies before you buy.

- Ask for confirmation of your order. At the very least, save and print the order screen when you make your purchase.

- Use your common sense. Be suspicious of incredible offers. Be suspicious if the site features lots of screaming CAPITALS! Be suspicious of shops that operate off pages set up homepage networks like Geocities or Tripod – it's a sign that they might be a dodgy, fly-by-night outfit.

- Take it slow. Net shops remove the barriers that slow us down in the real world. In a way, that's the point. But sometimes, hauling your purchase to the checkout allows time for you to decide you don't want it. Sometimes it pays to hang back a bit.

It's worth visiting the pages on net shopping put up by The Office of Fair Trading **http://www.oft.gov.uk/html/shopping/index2.html**. There's some good basic advice, along with details on your legal rights when you buy on the net and what to do if things go wrong.

So where should you shop online? The best places to go to find out about net shops are the big online shopping directories, where you'll find reviews and links to the sites. The following are all worth a look:

ShopSmart – **http://www.shopsmart.com**

Shops on the Net – **http://www.shopsonthenet.co.uk**

Guardian Unlimited Shopping – **http://shopping.guardian.co.uk**

Which? Magazine's Webtrader page – **http://www.which.net/webtrader**

Strictly speaking, the latter is not a directory. In order to boost consumer confidence in net shopping, *Which? Magazine* runs a scheme that checks out online traders to see if they meet certain standards. If you then have problems with one of the shops they've approved, *Which?* will offer legal support and help. There are now so many shops signed up to the scheme that the pages covering it are now a kind of alternative shopping directory. The big ISPs, search sites and software companies also have shopping areas on their homepages. These are worth a browse. But remember that the sites you see here are the ones who have signed deals with the companies behind the homepage. You're not seeing everything the net has to offer.

Supermarket shopping on the net

As mentioned before, supermarket shopping is one of the biggest growth areas in online retail. Tesco has led the way, but the other big names are following. The advantages of getting someone else to do your weekly shop for you are obvious. However, it isn't without problems.

- It takes a while to get started – you need to set up your standard shopping list at first.
- The people who put your orders together don't always look at sell-by dates as carefully as you do.
- If a product you want is unavailable, the replacements they choose can be rather novel.

But overall, it's definitely worth a try. Visit the website of your favourite supermarket and see if they cover your area.

Kids and shopping

At the height of the whole dot.com boom, a few sites offering special shopping services for kids began to appear. Parents were supposed to set up an account at the site. Their kids could then use it buy things online. I don't think these sites really caught on – certainly you don't hear much about them these days. I'm not sure that they were a good idea anyway. Setting up an account involved a fair amount of effort. It was probably quicker and easier for parents to let their kids browse standard web shops, then get online and buy the things they found for them. A more useful service now offered by some of the bigger net shops (e.g. Amazon) is the wish list. The idea here is that as you browse a shop, you can add the things you want to a 'wish list'. People can then see what you want and buy it for you. OK, it rather takes the romance out of present-buying. But stressed-out relatives looking to placate grumpy teenagers probably don't care about romance. So it might come in handy.

Net shopping abroad

It's easy to browse net shops in the US and elsewhere. Actually buying something is more complicated, but there are lots of reasons to give it a go.

- Sometimes American net shops are the only place to go for some items – a book or CD yet to come out over here, a hard-to-get Christmas toy.

- Many products – books, CDs and computer software and hardware – are cheaper in the States, even after you take shipping costs and duty into account.

In general, shopping overseas requires a little care. Look around in the Help sections before you hit that *BUY* button.

- Check shipping costs and times carefully – there's no point in ordering that sought-after toy if it's going to arrive after Christmas.

- Some shops attach conditions to international orders (e.g. you have to spend over a certain amount). Some won't actually sell to overseas customers.

- Check whether guarantees on products apply abroad.

- Check on formats (US videos use the NTSC format, whereas here we use the PAL format) and sizes (American clothes sizes are different to ours).

- Incidentally, to keep track of how much you're spending, use the Universal Currency Converter **http://www.xe.net/ucc**.

What you pay at an American site isn't the end of it. You will probably pay more when your goods enter the country. There are three basic charges on goods imported into the UK – customs duty, excise duty and VAT. VAT is charged at 17.5%. Duty rates vary from product to product: they can go up to 15% of purchase price. However, there are all sorts of exemptions. There's a useful guide to the rates at the HM Customs & Excise website **http://www.hmce.gov.uk/bus/regions/dutyrate.htm**. You can find detailed information about the whole system in Notice 143 **http://www.hmce.gov.uk/notices/143.htm**. The Post Office are supposed to collect duty/VAT on delivery. They may also charge you 'a clearance fee' for collecting them, but often they don't get round to collecting any of these various charges. If you get something sent by one of the big international courier firms, they may collect the duty/VAT instead (and may charge more than the Post Office).

....
Shopping bots
....

There are various search tools – usually referred to as shopping bots – that will, in theory, find the lowest price online for a particular item. Shopsmart **http://www.shopsmart.com** has a useful shopping bot, as does Kelkoo **http://uk.kelkoo.com/**. DealTime's price comparison service is available at Guardian Unlimited Shopping **http://www.guardian.dealtime.co.uk/**. If you do use these:

- Check the number of shops that a particular bot searches. Some bot sites have deals with certain retailers and only search those pages, missing out cheaper competitors.

- Check whether the price served up by the bot includes shipping. If it doesn't, the results may be misleading. The better bots give you all the information you need to make a purchase, including delivery time.

- Some shopping bot sites don't update their price comparison databases as often as they should. So it can pay to hunt around on your own after you've done a price search.

....
Research it online, buy it offline
....

The net is a great tool for researching offline purchases. You can read product reviews online and check out the prices on offer, then head down the high street better equipped to get a good deal. The UK is yet to catch up with the States in this area. But there's more and more information online:

- You can read some of *Which? Magazine*'s product tests at **http://www.which.net**.

- Many specialist consumer magazines are now on the net, from hi-fi guides like *What Hi-Fi* **http://www.whathifi.com** to car-buying magazines like *AutoExpress* **http://www.autoexpress.co.uk** and *What Car* **http://www.whatcar.co.uk**.

- Some publishers now pool the reviews from their magazines on their sites – try ZD Net **http://www.zdnet.co.uk** for some useful help with computer buying.

- Some sites try to locate the best real-world prices for certain items – for example Buy.co.uk **http://www.buy.co.uk** has tools that help you find the cheapest rates for gas, electricity and water in your area.

Classified ads are another good source for bargains. They're moving online, where they make a lot more sense. Once they're put into a database, ads are a lot easier to search. You can also set up search tools that send you email alerts when an ad for something you want appears online. Once you find an ad, you contact the seller as usual, either by telephone or email. Many of the big classified ad outlets are online, from the general – *Loot* **http://www.loot.com** and *Exchange and Mart* **http://www.exchangeandmart.co.uk** – to the specialist: *Autotrader* **http://www.autotrader.co.uk**. Several online operations have also moved into the area – for example, Yahoo! runs a classified section **http://uk.classifieds.yahoo.com/uk**.

Online auctions

Over the last few years, buying and selling at online auctions has become one of the most popular activities on the net. Log on to eBay **http://www.ebay.com**, the place where it all got started (the UK end is at **http://www.ebay.co.uk**), and you'll see millions of auctions in progress – individuals selling everything from remaindered computer parts to modern-day collectables like *Star Wars* and Beanie Babies. Imagine a global car boot sale and you come close to understanding what's going on here. Unsurprisingly, eBay's success has led to others setting up auctions. EBay's competitors include:

Freeserve **http://669.fairmarket.co.uk/**

Yahoo! **http://uk.auctions.yahoo.com/uk/**

Amazon **http://www.amazon.co.uk**

QXL **http://www.qxl.com**

eBid **http://www.ebid.co.uk**

Loot **http://auction.loot.com/scripts/lootsite.dll**

It's easy to see why net auctions are so popular. They do the thing the net was always supposed to do – they allow people with similar interests to pursue those interests together. At their best, they create genuine communities. And they're fun. Seeing the incredible prices at the start of auctions, you can't help but be drawn in.

In online auctions, you can either buy direct from the site hosting the sale or from another individual. Bids are sent in via the net and auctions are time-limited, In other words, products go to the person who gets the highest bid in before the deadline. Often people wait until the last minute and things can get a bit hectic. When buying at an auction site:

- Check on exactly what you're buying. That super-cheap computer is probably second-hand or end-of-the-line stock.

- If you're buying from an individual, check on their past performance. EBay and QXL post reports on sellers from previous buyers, so you can see how they behaved and whether the goods were sent on time.

- Find out what the item you're bidding on is actually worth. Auctions specialize in items that are hard to price exactly. So you'll need to think about what the thing is actually worth to you.

- Set a price you're willing to pay and stick to it. It's easy to get carried away and end up paying way over the odds (that's why sellers like them, despite those apparently low prices).

- Finally, if you're buying from an individual on an auction site, use an escrow service. Most big auction sites run them. The buyer pays by credit card into a special 'escrow account'. The auction site then tells the seller that the money is there. It stays there until the buyer gets the goods. Once the buyer confirms that the goods have arrived and are as described, the money is released to the seller.

Creating your own homepage

There is a tendency among the established media to see personal homepages as the preserve of cranks. Apparently, the websites put up by committed amateurs are full of half-baked theories, spelling mistakes and bad graphics, and just can't compete with the high tech, zippily animated efforts of established names and big companies. Complete rubbish. A good webpage doesn't need anything more than some well thought-out words in a row. A good eye when it comes to laying them out won't hurt, but the multimedia gimmicks definitely aren't necessary. In fact, many big names spend so much time worrying about the flashy gimmicks that they never get round to producing any worthwhile content behind them. The truth is that motivated amateurs create some of the best websites. And more than a few of those motivated amateurs are teenage kids.

How putting up a homepage can benefit your family:

- Your kids will get a real sense of achievement from doing it. It really isn't hard to get something decent up and running online. It will be a way for your kids to express themselves creatively and they may end up producing something that compares very favourably with the efforts of the professionals.

- Putting up a homepage about a particular interest is a great way to connect with people who share that interest. Putting up a page about a particular club or school team can help publicize what they're up to. It can give a focus to the team/club's activities.

Potential problems with putting up a homepage that parents should be aware of:

- Your kids can tell the world what they think via their homepage.

Fine. But you need to teach them not to give away important information – their home address, telephone number and so on. There are people who might try to abuse this information. Your kids need to be careful with email addresses too. Don't put your main account address on your homepage. You never know who might get hold of it. In general, be careful when it comes to the information you put on kids' homepages – think a bit before giving details about schools/clubs and before putting up photos of kids.

• Webpages that become popular can cause problems. If your kids have created a site about a popular film/book/cartoon or toy, you and they may receive letters and visits from copyright lawyers insisting you have impinged on their client's brand equity or something. This kind of thing is pretty shortsighted, but it has happened. If a personal page becomes very popular, the site hosting it (your ISP, for example) may close it down because of the excess traffic, or start charging you.

Getting started

So what do you need to put up your own page? Nothing apart from your browser. You can put up a webpage very quickly while online at one of the big community sites like Yahoo! Geocities **http://geocities.yahoo.com.home** and Tripod **http://www.tripod.com** and some of the family homepage sites mentioned below. Once you've registered and filled out a couple of forms, you can use templates on the site to create a page in a matter of minutes. This can be a great way for kids to get started. Even younger children will be able to sort something out with your help. Remember to make sure they don't put up personal/private information.

> **Web bugs on homepages** When you put up a quick page on some of the web community sites, these sites will sometimes, without your knowledge or consent, add a small program known as a web bug to the page. This then tracks people who visit your site, sending information about what they do online to other companies (often market research operations). The companies behind this kind of thing say they don't collect 'personally identifiable information' on the people who visit your page. Still, the covert nature of the whole thing might affect whether you want to use these services.

If you and your kids want to put up a more complex pages, the best way is to create your site on your home PC and then upload it to the web once you've finished. To do this, you need:

- **Some web publishing software** There are plenty of easily available web publishing software packages that make the whole process as simple as creating word-processor documents.

- **An online home** It's easy to get free space for your page – either on your ISP's site or on one of the web communities like Yahoo! Geocities or Tripod.

- **A scanner** There are lots of graphics available for free online, but if you want to put lots of your own photos on your page, a scanner will come in handy.

If you get serious about your site, you'll eventually need a decent FTP client. Browsers are OK for downloads but if you're going to be uploading regularly to your own pages, something like Cute FTP **http://www.cuteftp.com** will be useful. If you want to do some sort of cutting-edge multimedia extravaganza, you'll have to learn some more complex programming and/ or buy some fairly expensive software. But if your kids just want to share their thoughts on S Club 7 with the world, you'll probably have the software you need already and won't need to do that much research.

....

HTML basics

....

HTML is the language used to create webpages. Basically, it's a set of text commands – known as tags – which determine the way a document is laid out, the line spacing, placement of images, links to other documents and much else. When a document written in HTML is viewed by a browser, you see the content the way the designer intended. If you open the same document in a text editor, you see all the tags around the basic content. Actually, you can view the HTML code for any webpage you're browsing:

- **In Internet Explorer:**
  Select the *VIEW* menu, then *SOURCE*.

- **In Netscape 6**
  Select the *VIEW* menu then *PAGE SOURCE*.

As you'll see, tags are enclosed by < and >. You may also notice that they generally come in pairs – an opening and a closing tag. The closing tag usually features a forward slash, as in **</BOLD>**. Looking at the source code of webpages can give you a few clues about how to use HTML. However, there are several useful interactive tutorials online which let you mess around with tags and see what they do.

- HotWired does a good introductory tutorial on its web developer site WebMonkey **http://www.hotwired.com/webmonkey/teachingtool/**.

- For more in-depth information, try the NCSA's Beginner's Guide to HTML **http://www.ncsa.uiuc.edu/General/Internet/WWW/HTMLPrimerP1.html**.

- For a good general introduction to webpage design, try the HTML Headquarters **http://webhelp.org**.

- Mike Smith's Guide to HTML and CGI Scripts is worth a look **http://snowwhite.it.brighton.ac.uk/~mas/mas/courses/html/html.html**.

- Big Nose Bird also has some useful advice **http://www.bignosebird.com/**.

....

HTML editors

....

Beginners don't really need to bother learning HTML. There are plenty of WYSIWYG programs (as in 'what you see is what you get') that let you design webpages without ever having to expose yourself to any techno gobbledegook. Professional designers argue that you shouldn't rely on these editors because they don't create 'clean' HTML, and that in the end you have to sort out the mistakes they introduce. But this isn't really an issue for most ordinary users: they just want something that's easy to use. So what should you try?

- The latest versions of Word, Microsoft's word processing package, features webpage templates you can adapt. It also lets you create documents the way you would normally, then save them as HTML.

- You should have received something you can use when you downloaded your browser. Internet Explorer comes with Front Page Express. Netscape 6 has Composer. Both are fine if you're just starting out.

There are plenty of specialist HTML editors/web publishing packages you could also look at:

Hot Dog Pro **http://www.sausagetools.com**

Hot Metal Pro **http://www.hotmetalpro.com/**

Arachnophilia **http://www.arachnoid.com/arachnophilia/index.html**

Coffee cup HTML Editor **http://www.coffeecup.com**

Mac users could try BBEdit **http://www.barebones.com**

For creating and formatting the visual content of your page (the graphics should be saved as gifs and any photos as jpegs), try Paint Shop Pro **http://www.jasc.com**.

Many professional designers use Macromedia'sDreamweaver **http://www.macromedia.com/software/dreamweaver/**. In the past, *.net* magazine has given away outdated versions of Dreamweaver on their cover discs).

Making the page

When it comes to learning how to use your web publishing package, the best thing is to play around and try things out. Read the Help files if you get stuck. To be honest, though, mastering the technology isn't the real problem when it comes to creating a webpage. Things will work a lot better if you think a bit about what you want your page to say before you get started. So encourage your kids to:

• Think about what they want to talk about on their homepage. A page can be about their friends and family. It can be about anything they're interested in – their favourite film or book, their pets, their collections, the sports team they're in. Get your kids to pick a subject, then think about what they want to say about it.

- Think about how the page will look. What kind of graphics do you want to include? There are websites where you can download web graphics for free – more on these shortly. You could also put up your own photos, but you'll need to scan them in and save them in the right format.

- Plan the page out on a bit of paper. Think about how the pages will link together. Don't aim too high at the start. It's fine to put up a single page at first, then build other pages around it.

When your and your kids start to construct the page on the computer, there are a few things to consider:

- Keep the text you write short and sweet. Don't put up great long essays that take a lot of scrolling through. You want people to get the basic idea from what they see when the page first loads on the screen. Make sure you spell-check what you write.

- Think about how people are going to view your page. That big graphic file/photo of the family dog may look like the perfect front page from where you're sitting, but if it takes several minutes to load nobody is going to hang around to see the rest of your site. If you do want to put up big photos, put them on a separate page and warn people about possible delays when the page loads.

- If you're just putting up a page of links to your favourite *Harry Potter* sites, navigation – how people move around your site – won't be an issue. If you put up a group of pages, you'll need to think about it. Whatever you do, at least make sure that on every page you always include a link back to your front page. That way people can get back to the beginning quickly if they get lost.

- Back in the early days of the web, people often rushed up pages that weren't finished. Web surfers got used to clicking links promising great things and finding blank pages that were 'under construction'. This isn't the greatest crime you can commit when you're putting together a page. But try to avoid it if possible.

When it comes to the general design of your page, it can help to have a look at the pages other people have put up. If you want to get really technical, you could look at the source of pages you particularly like to see how the designers achieved a particular effect. But don't just steal any good ideas you find. Look and learn by all means. But try to adapt what you find. Kids may find it helpful and inspiring to look at the pages put up by other children. Try the following sites:

Web Kids' Village
http://www.ks-connection.org/village/village.html

Yahooligans http://www.yahooligans.com

My Family http://www.myfamily.com

Family Shoebox http://www.familyshoebox.com

Some people suggest that you can learn about web design by looking at bad webpages, although what constitutes a badly designed webpage is still open to argument. Your snidey teenagers might get something out of a site like Web Pages That Suck **http://www.webpagesthatsuck.com** though it's probably not for younger kids.

Teenage kids who get serious about their sites can get lots of useful design advice online from the following sites:

Webmonkey
http://hotwired.lycos.com/webmonkey/design/index.html

Philip Greenspun http://philip.greenspun.com/, author of the excellent Philip and Alex's Guide to Web Publishing
http://www.arsdigita.com/books/panda/

Lynda Weinman http://www.lynda.com/, a much-respected American web designer

The Useable Web directory http://usableweb.com/ has tips on making your site more user-friendly. There's more of the same at Useit.com **http://www.useit.com/**, the site put up by interface theorist Jakob Nielsen.

The various net magazines, in particular, *.net* and *Internet Magazine*, are useful sources of both software and website design tips. If you're really serious, try the sites aimed at professional web designers. They can be good places to find out what's new. Try HotWired's WebMonkey **http://hotwired.lycos.com/webmonkey/**, CNet's Builder.com **http://www.builder.com** or Website Garage **http://websitegarage.netscape.com/**.

There are sites where you can download free graphics – everything from buttons and icons to backgrounds and general images. There are even sites where you can pick up free tools you can use to add features to your page – everything from discussion groups to search engines. Have a look at the following:

ClipArt **http://www.clipart.com** Loads of free images and graphics you can use to pretty up your page.

Elated **http://www.elated.com/** You'll find useful advice and some free graphics here.

Free Find **http://www.freefind.com** Tips on adding a search engine to your site.

Free Graphics **http://www.freegraphics.com** It does what it says on the tin – lots of free bits of art to use on your site.

IconBazaar **http://www.iconbazaar.com** Find lots of useful navigational graphics here – arrows, buttons, pointers and the like.

Excite UK has some useful links to more sites offering this kind of thing at **http://www.excite.co.uk/computers_and_internet/directory/310132/310148/189743/**.

Another 'design' issue you may ultimately want to think about is your domain name. If you put your page on your ISP's site (or on a site like Yahoo! Geocities), you'll be lumbered with a long, rather clumsy web address – something like **http://www.yourisp.net/freespace/yourname/**. Your pages will have more impact – and will be easier to find – if you have your own snappy domain name. Your ISP will probably be able to help you register something appropriate. Alternatively try Net Names **http://www.netnames.co.uk**. You could try using V3 Redirect Services **http://come.to/**. They help you to set up a more interesting name and then redirect the traffic to your site.

Publishing and publicizing your page

Once you've laid out your masterwork, you need to upload it to your ISP's server or to the site hosting your page. Get in touch with your ISP to find out exactly how to do this. In fact, it's worth talking to them about your page in general. Though all the ISPs now offer free space for webpages, they have lots of little rules that may come into effect if, for example, your page turns out to be either controversial or incredibly popular. Once your page is up, tell your friends and family. How about telling the rest of the world it's out there?

- You can submit the details of your page to the major search engines, though this can be time-consuming. There are sites that let you submit the details to all the engines at once – try Submit It **http://www.submit-it.com** or the Submission Wizard at Exploit **http://www.exploit.com**.

- If your kids belong to a particular mailing list or discussion group, they could send them details of their page. But be wary of sending anything that resembles spam.

- If your child's site is about a popular topic, they could try joining the web ring devoted to that subject – for more on web rings, go back to the section on search engines on page 80.

- If your page features links to their favourite sites, try getting in touch with them and see if they'll put in a link to your page. If they do, it might drive some traffic your way.

Faster connections

If your family really gets into the net, you may want to move to a faster connection. A few years ago, that meant getting an ISDN line, a digital telephone line that offers connection speeds of up to 128 Kbps. ISDN lets you do two things at once. You can be connected to the net and talking on the telephone at the same time, all via the same line. BT tried hard to sell ISDN to ordinary users via its Home Highway service, but it never really caught on with home users. You needed extra hardware, set-up and installation were expensive, and rental and call charges weren't cheap either. Now you don't really need to bother with it. Your two main choices are ADSL and cable.

ADSL

ADSL (Asymmetric Digital Subscriber Line) uses a standard telephone line to deliver a high speed connection to the net – speeds on offer can go up to 2Mb a second – that's around forty times faster than a 56K modem. You pay a flat monthly fee and get a connection to the net that is 'always on'. In other words, when you want to get online, you don't need to make a dial-up connection. You're there already, as it were. The highest-profile ADSL service currently on offer comes from BT. Find out more at **http://www.btopenworld.com/**. With most ADSL services, you pay an installation charge, then a flat monthly fee. There are various things you need to think about before you sign up:

- You need a reasonably up-to-date computer (one running Windows 98 or Mac OS 8.1 or higher).

- You need new bits of kit, in particular an ADSL modem. Often the hardware you need is included in the installation charge.

- With some services, you need to sign up for a minimum of twelve months.

- To get it, your local exchange needs to be ADSL-enabled. Your line will need to pass a line test.

- ADSL is distance-dependent. If you're too far away, it degrades considerably. So you need to live within 1–3 miles of your exchange.

BT's is the highest-profile ADSL service currently on offer. But other ISPs are moving into the market. Find out more at ADSL Guide **http://www.adslguide.org.uk**.

Cable

Cable can deliver fantastic connection speeds – up to 10Mbps in both directions. Unfortunately, the network is still being built and coverage can be patchy – you'll probably be fine if you live in or near a big city. The main players in the UK are NTL **http://www.ntl.co.uk** and Telewest **http://www.telewest.co.uk**, via their Blue Yonder service. Again, there are several things you need to think about.

- You need a reasonably up-to-date PC or Mac.

- You'll also need new hardware – a cable modem and an Ethernet Card.

- You share a cable with your neighbours. So if everyone uses the service at the same time, download speeds can fall drastically.

Things change constantly in the internet access business. For up-to-date information on cable deals – everything from prices to which companies have entered the market, try The Cable Modem Centre **http://www.cable-modems.co.uk/**.

Security and 'always-on' broadband connections Because broadband connections are always on, they are more vulnerable to potential intruders than the standard dial-up connection. Your ISP can help configure your computer so that it is more secure during installation. You can also block potential intruders by installing a firewall – try Zone Alarm **http://www.zonealarm.com**.

4

Essential clicks for kids

helping your children make
the most of the net

We've now got to a stage where everything that happens in the real world is represented in some way online. Whatever your children's interests are, whether they're mad about animals or Atomic Kitten, they'll be able to follow up those interests on the net. How best can you help? Sometimes, the best thing is just to get out there and surf and search with them. If something catches your kids' interest (for example, a particular book or a nature documentary on TV), try using a search engine and/or a child-friendly directory to see if you can find out more. There's advice about this on page 71. But here's a quick reminder of some of the potential problems to look out for with net searching.

- Vague search terms will not only yield links that have nothing much to do with the thing you're looking for. They may also turn up adult material you don't want your children to access (combining the search terms 'girls' and 'toys', for example, might not deliver quite the results you expect).

- Some search sites, if they think you're searching for adult material, will put ads for porn sites on the page of results that they deliver.

- Some porn webmasters try to con search sites by putting popular references (Digimon, Britney Spears and so on) in the 'meta tags' used to identify/categorize pages by the programs that assemble search engine databases. Their idea is to get their sites onto more search engine results screens and hence accessed by more people. The ultimate aim is to rake in more money for the advertising banners on their pages.

- Some porn webmasters also register domain names associated with celebrities, again in the hope of drawing more traffic and thus making more money from advertising.

The solutions to these problems are relatively simple:

- Use a kids-only search engine or directory – something like Ask Jeeves for Kids, AOL Search – Kids Only or Yahooligans. These will only serve up child-friendly results/ads. You'll find the web addresses in the Resources section of the Essential Clicks for Kids Directory that follows shortly.

- If you do want to use a more general search engine, pick one that lets you set up a family filter that will block adult results and ads – Google, Alta Vista or Lycos, for example. Again, you'll find the addresses in the Resources section of the Directory.

Age guidelines and online projects

As mentioned before, this is a net manual, not a parenting book. The idea is to help you use the net, not to tell you how best to raise your kids. That said, a few suggestions about which net activities are appropriate for different age groups may come in handy. But remember – these are just suggestions. All kids are different. Some may be comfortable online from an early age. Others may never really get the net at all.

0–6 years

The net is not really for younger children. To use it properly, you need to be able to read and write (and type). When you introduce your kids to the net is up to you. But don't force it on them too early. Thanks to all the idealistic hype about the educational power of the net, some parents think they have to get their kids surfing before they're out of nappies. I have my doubts about this. It's perfectly possible to find sites online that will interest 2–3 year-olds, but most toddlers get frustrated by the delays that are still part of the online experience. Very young children will probably get more out of multimedia CD-ROMs. That said, older children in this age group will enjoy surfing with you and may be more willing to put up with delays and lengthy download times.

Here are a few activities children in this age group might enjoy:

• **Search the web** This may sound obvious, but simply following up their interests online can be fascinating for this age group. It will introduce them to the net, show how it works and the amount of stuff that's out there. Do the searching, but once you find an appropriate site, let them click round it and explore.

- **Look for the website for your kids' favourite book/TV show/film/toy** These sites usually feature all sorts of related content you can download – songs, stories, pictures they can print out and colour in. For example, you'll find sites for *Teletubbies* and *The Tweenies* at BBC Online. Just go to the CBBC (Children's BBC) homepage at **http://www.bbc.co.uk/cbbc/** and look for the relevant links.

- **Send an e-card to relatives** Writing emails will be a little beyond this age group. But electronic greetings cards are a lot easier. You just have to choose from various options then press *SEND*. Some sites also let users customize standard designs. The selection at KidsCom is a good starting point: **http://www.kidscom.com/orakc/cards/index.html**.

- **Play a game** The websites created for the big name cartoons/films often feature little games created using Shockwave/Flash. Some can take a while to download, but when they're done your child can get on and play with no further delays. You'll find games featuring Scooby Doo, Daffy Duck and more on the Cartoon Network site at **http://www.cartoonnetwork.com/games**.

- **Read a comic** Most online comics use Shockwave/Flash and are like a cross between a print comic and a full-blown cartoon. They still feature text, though, so they may be a good way of encouraging older children in this age group to practice reading. Your kids will probably enjoy what's on offer from Disney at **http://www.disney.co.uk/DisneyOnline/Stories/index_flash.html**.

- **Get a bird's eye view of your home** If you live in a big city, at Multimap **http://www.multimap.com** you can type in your address and they'll bring up an overhead photo of your neighbourhood that your kids can then print out.

- **Watch a webcam** Many webcams feature rather dubious material. But there are plenty that are eminently suitable for kids. Simply looking at locations on the other side of the world from your own home can be enthralling. Alternatively, looking at places online that you've been to in real life can be interesting. Try the Yahooligans webcam page **http://www.yahooligans.com/content/wc/**

- **Listen to a story online** Many sites now feature readings from well-known children's books. Quality isn't always great, but they might fill the odd hour. You can listen to selected nursery rhymes, various Beatrix Potter stories and *Alice in Wonderland* at the Kids' Corner site **http://www.tcom.ohiou.edu/books/kids.htm**.

- **Put your kids' paintings online** You'll need a scanner, unless you've got a computer art program and your kids create something directly on the screen. But there are lots of sites that showcase kids' pictures. Try Art Kids **http://www.artkids.co.uk/home.htm**.

- **Download a dinosaur** Or rather, download and print out various paper dinosaurs you can then assemble using scissors and glue. You'll find lots of designs at **http://www.rain.org/~philfear/download-a-dinosaur.html**.

Kids' multimedia If you're looking for some advice about good kids' multimedia CD-ROMs, try the excellent Parents Information Network **http://www.pin.org.uk/**, where you'll find reviews of kids' software by teachers and parents. The site also has useful advice about net filtering software, internet safety and much more. If you want to buy PIN's recommendations online, try Learning Store **http://www.learningstore.co.uk** or Amazon **http://www.amazon.co.uk**.

7–12 years

The net really comes into its own for the kids that marketers call 'tweens'. Once they can read/write/type, they can take control a bit more online. The web and email are likely to prove most useful for the 7–12s. They'll be able to search the web themselves, either to pursue their own hobbies or interests, or for homework assignments. They can also start sending emails to friends and family members. As kids in this age group get closer to teenage, they may want to try chat and discussion groups. These activities may prove frustrating if attempted too early. In particular, to chat well, you need to be a reasonable typist. You won't always need to help 'tweens' find the information they want, but you can start teaching them net literacy – how to navigate a site, how to assess the information they find, how to spot ads and so on.

Here are a few activities children in this age group might enjoy:

- **Research their family tree online** The net has been embraced wholeheartedly by genealogists and there are now all sorts of resources available online for those who want to dig around in their family roots. Try RootsWeb **http://www.rootsweb.com**, **http://www.genuki.org.uk** or **http://www.origins.net**.

- **Send email to relatives who are online** Once kids can write/type, why not help them to send mail to cousins and grandparents? Email can also make sending 'thank you' notes after birthdays and Christmas seem less painless to kids who are keen to get on with playing with their presents.

- **Join an online pen pal programme** The net makes exchanging mail with children in other countries easier than it's ever been. That said, there are dangers. There is evidence that some adults try to get on to pen pal programmes that aren't properly monitored. To keep things safe, do things via your child's school. You'll find advice and links at ePals **http://www.epals.com**.

- **Download software** There are a huge number of free downloads for kids available online – everything from games and educational software to screensavers and art programs. For an introduction to what's out there, try the freeware programs made available by Grey Olltwit at **http://www.adders.org/freeware/index.html**.

- **Get help with video games** There are loads of games sites online, many aimed at adults and/or children older than this age group, so you may need to take some care here. But if your child gets stuck on a particular game, they can find 'walkthroughs' online that will help them negotiate difficult levels. Try Gamespot **http://www.gamespot.co.uk** and Games Domain **http://www.gamesdomain.co.uk/cheats/index.html**.

- **Look after a virtual pet** Lots of sites let users either 'adopt' virtual cats/dogs or create their own cyber-critters and then look after them. Kids might enjoy this and it will be a lot less messy than the real thing, obviously. Try Virtual Puppy **http://www.virtualpuppy.com** or NeoPets **http://www.neopets.com**.

- **Chat to a chatbot** Chatting can be tricky for this age group – that's chatting with a human. Chatting with a machine can be a little easier. There are lots of chatbots online – automated programs that respond to typed queries and attempt to simulate a conversation. Try Alicebot **http://www.alicebot.org** or some of the commercial programs mentioned on Agentland **http://www.agentland.com**.

- **Help mum and dad find old school friends** Using the net to reconnect with people you used to know is one of the big online fads of the moment. Sites like Friends Reunited **http://www.friendsreunited.co.uk** help you to track down the people you used to go to school with. It might amuse your kids to do this kind of search with you.

- **Help set up a family photo album online** Some photo websites will develop standard film and show the results online. Once it's there, friends and family can also view the images, once you give

them your password. This could be a good way of sharing snaps from a birthday party or other special occasion with distant family members. Try Boots' web photo service at
http://www.bootsphoto.com.

• **Put their stories online** ABC Tales showcases writing – fiction and non-fiction – by ordinary people. As this book was going to press, it was planning to open a special site for kids to do the same. Go to **http://www.abctales.com** and look for the appropriate links.

13–16 years

When kids reach teenage, they're more than capable of using the net themselves. Chat and instant messaging are particularly popular with this age group. Online gaming is also gaining ground with teenage boys. Teens may be drawn to experimenting some of the dodgier things online – from accessing sites with content you don't approve of (porn, gory pictures, crackpot conspiracy theories and so on) to swapping illegal MP3 music files. Superficially, this age group starts to outpace their parents online. They can seem a lot more net-savvy. But just because they know about the latest hot net fad and you don't doesn't mean that your experience and advice won't come in handy. So try to keep abreast of what your kids do online. Don't let the net become something they do in isolation. Keep advising them on net literacy. Try to encourage them to do other, more creative things online apart from just hanging out in chatrooms.

Here are a few activities children in this age group might enjoy:

• **Create their own website** Teenagers always go on about needing their own space. So why not encourage them to create their own homepage? It's easy to do something very simple, by using the online templates available at Yahoo! Geocities **http://geocities.yahoo.com/home**, Tripod **http://www.tripod.com** and the other big homepage networks. But make sure they don't give away any important personal information via their site.

- **Create their own online club** Hanging out with friends is very important for teens. Via Yahoo! Clubs **http://uk.clubs.yahoo.com** they can create an online hangout where they can chat, swap ideas, share pictures and more with their chums.

- **Create a weblog** Add a little structure and purpose to your child's surfing by suggesting they do their own weblog. These are personal online journals, in which people pick out links to interesting sites, adding a few comments of their own. Many weblogs have a rather confessional feel. Others find links around a particular theme. I'd encourage your kids to go for the latter. That avoids the potential problems connected with children revealing personal information online. Free software that makes setting up a weblog pretty easy is available from Blogger **http://www.blogger.com**.

- **Download music files** Not all music circulating on the net is there illegally. Many artists make some tracks available for free. Your kids may be able to find music by their favourite artists on one of the big mainstream music portals – try Listen.com **http://www.listen.com** or Vitaminic **http://www.vitaminic.com/main**.

- **Chat to your favourite celeb** Many big websites host chats with celebrities – actors, pop stars, film directors. The BBC **http://www.bbc.co.uk** and Channel 4 **http://www.channel4.com** often follow up shows with live online chats with the people involved. This could be a good way of getting teens out of the same old chatrooms.

- **Sell off your old toys** If your teenage kids don't want their bedrooms cluttered up with their old Star Wars figures and Barbies, they could try selling them online at eBay **http://www.ebay.co.uk**. Some old toys are particularly sought after by collectors.

- **Make their own dance tracks** There are all sorts of music-making programs available online. Propellerheads Software **http://www.propellerheads.se** have developed a variety of music creation tools, from synthesizer emulators to samplers. The demo versions are generally available for free – with 'Rebirth' and 'Recycle', in particular, your kids could easily knock out their own house/techno tunes.

- **Help in the search for intelligent life on other planets** If you download a screensaver from SETI@Home **http://setiathome.ssl.berkeley.edu**, it will let SETI (Search for Extra-Terrestrial Intelligence) use your computer's power when you're not. The idea is to pool the power of net-connected PCs round the world to create a distributed computer that can analyze radio signals from space for evidence of alien communication. If this doesn't interest your teenage kids, they might prefer Parabon **http://www.parabon.com**, who use similar methods to do research into potential cures for cancer.

- **Predict the future** Predicting the future and generally messing around with the various ways people have used to guess at what's round the corner are popular with teens. There are lots of things they can fool around with online, from Virtual Ouija board and web-based Tarot readings to online I-Ching readings. Go to **http://www.yahooligans.com/Computers__Games__and_Online/Online _Games/Prediction_Games** for some useful links.

- **Waste lots of time at Sodaplay** One of the most amusingly pointless ways of passing time online is the Sodaconstructor, which lets you create little animated models out of simple lines. Sounds like nothing much, but it is strangely compelling. At Sodaplay **http://www.sodaplay.com**, your kids can create their own models, send them to friends and see what others have done.

Directory of essential clicks for kids

The best way to find the things you want online is usually to go looking for them yourself. That said, there's so much online that it's easy to get, if not lost, then sidetracked. That's where the following directory of sites should come in handy. Some people reckon that this kind of print directory doesn't really make sense. Online directories are usually more up to date, and can take you directly to the sites they cover, they say. True enough. Then again, print directories can help prepare you before you get online. They give you a quick idea of what's out there. That's the plan with the Essential Clicks for Kids, a short selection of some of the most popular/amusing/interesting websites for kids. The idea is to alert you to sites you might not know about or find if you were just clicking around online. Think of the following as a kind of Bookmarks/Favourites starter pack. As ever with the net, feel free to edit and add your own.

A quick note on how this directory is organised. When I was doing the initial research, the idea was to split it up into two distinct sections – one devoted to education, one to entertainment. When I came to put it together, that original dividing line began to blur a little and it seemed to make more sense to do a general directory. The whole thing starts with a section on generally useful sites, things like search engines, directories, kids' portals and download sites. As I began to put the directory together, I realized that most of the sites I was including were aimed primarily at the 7–12 age group. For that reason, I decided to include special sections highlighting some of the better sites for toddlers and teenagers. Finally, at the beginning of some sections, where it's appropriate, I've added some general advice about things to look out for.

Search sites

There are now a number of search engines and directories designed specifically for kids. The search engines automatically block all adult content. Similarly, the directories link only to appropriate material.

About.com Kids http://home.about.com/kids/. About.com is one of the more accessible directories, perhaps because it features reviews and links put together by people rather than machines. Their Kids section is very useful.

Ask Jeeves for Kids http://www.ajkids.com. The kids' version of the search engine that lets you ask questions in plain English. Lots of other useful content here.

AOL Search – Kids Only http://www.aol.co.uk/kids/netfind/. The big online service's own search engine for kids.

Berit's Best Sites for Children http://www.beritsbest.com/. Useful directory of 1,000 child-friendly links reviewed and rated by American librarian Berit Erickson. The 'Top 25 sites' section is very useful.

FIDO http://www.clark.net/pub/soh/fido.htm. The Family Internet Directory Online has five hundred useful links – pity about the design.

Kids Click http://www.kidsclick.org/. A comprehensive directory of child-friendly links assembled by more US librarians. No flashy graphics – just excellent content.

Kids Like It http://www.kidslikeit.co.uk/. UK directory of links put together by kids for kids.

Onekey http://www.onekey.com. A general search engine that sets out to be kid-friendly. There's a useful directory of links too.

UK Favourites for Kids http://www.ukfavouritesforkids.com/. Another useful UK kids' directory, assembled by one Betty Bookmark.

Yahooligans http://www.yahooligans.com. A kids' directory of links from Yahoo!, the leading general online directory. As good as you'd expect.

Filtered search engines

These are general search engines that let parents set up some kind of parental control or family filter which blocks adult content and ads.

Google **http://www.google.com**. Now the leading search engine. Their Kids' Directory **http://directory.google.com/Top/Kids_and_Teens/** is also worth a look.

AltaVista **http://www.av.com**. Still one of the big names in the search engine business. Look for the family filter link on the front page.

Lycos **http://searchguard.lycos.com/**. Another of the big names in net searching. This URL takes you direct to their family filter.

Lists of links

Where does a directory end and a list of links begin? Leave others to ponder this particular poser. Here are some more sites that will help you and your kids out:

American Library Association Cool Sites for Kids
http://www.ala.org/alsc/children_links.html. America's librarians are very active online – here are some more useful links to quality kids' content on the net.

Howard's Links 4 Kids
http://www.geocities.com/Heartland/1143/main.html. You see less of these one-person efforts online now – they used to be around a lot more in the early days. Still useful.

Interesting Places to Browse for Kids
http://interesting.places.to/Browse/forKids/. The web address says it all – a functional set of links but just as useful as some of the flashier efforts.

Launch Site http://www.launchsite.org/english/index.html. Another useful list of links, mainly to places where kids can meet and hang out together.

Net Mom http://www.netmom.com/. The online companion to the American print directory, *The Internet Kids and Family Yellow Pages*.

....

Kids' portals

....

'Portal' is one of those clumsy pieces of net slang loved by business types and disliked by everyone else. A portal is an all-purpose site that features search tools, discussion boards, chatrooms, places to put homepages and more. There are now more and more of these sites aimed specifically at kids. Many, though not all, are American. With some, you can also download filtering programs that help block inappropriate content. Others describe themselves as 'safe harbours' or 'safe havens' meaning that they only feature links to approved sites and that they host monitored/moderated chatrooms and discussion spaces.

Alfy http://www.alfy.com. A colourful 'online playground' aimed at 3–9 year-olds, this includes games, links, cartoons, toys and more.

AtKidz http://www.atkidz.com/home/index.html. UK kids' site aimed at pre-teens and teens, with chat, free email, game tips and more. Parents can also download net filtering software here.

Bonus http://www.bonus.com. Flashy cartoony site aimed at the older end of the 7–12 group. Lots of games and pop gossip.

Cyberkids http://www.cyberkids.com/. A place online for kids to share art, ideas and more. Aimed mainly at 7–12s.

Headbone http://www.headbone.com. Aimed at 8–14 year-olds, this slick but safety-conscious site has instant messaging, multi-player games and monitored chatrooms.

International Kids' Space http://www.kids-space.org/. Another place where kids from around the world can share art, stories and music.

Kids Channel http://www.kids-channel.co.uk. UK safe haven for kids, with games, stories, colouring and a 'sell or swap' area.

KidsCom http://www.kidscom.com/. A safe educational playground for kids from 4–15, apparently. Lots of good content and games, and clever features, as in the Ad Bug, which appears alongside all banner ads to make sure kids know what they are.

KidLink http://www.kidlink.org/english/general/intro.html. A site that aims to bring together kids from around the world, this has monitored / controlled IRC chat, discussions and mailing lists.

KidsLink http://www.kidslink.co.uk/. Another 'safe haven', mainly featuring loads of links. Possibly not updated that often.

Kids' Place http://www.eduplace.com/kids/index.html. Games, quizzes and other content, mostly with an educational twist – all ad-free, apparently, which is a bonus.

Kid World http://www.bconnex.net/~kidworld/index.html. Another site created by kids, for kids apparently. Stories, jokes, games and more.

Lycos Zone http://www.lycoszone.com/. The search engine company's bright and breezy site for 7–12s, with games, homework help, survey and much more.

Our Kids http://www.ourkids.org.uk/. UK-created safe haven site with games, galleries, clubs, e-cards and more.

Planet Kids http://www.planetkids.co.uk. Very flashy kids' destination site with links to all sorts of other sites.

Squigly's Playhouse http://www.squiglysplayhouse.com/. Low-tech but still effective kids' portal where kids can swap stories, jokes, brain-teasers and more.

Surf Monkey http://www.surfmonkey.com. All-purpose net safety service that not only filters content, but helps them communicate with friends in safety too. Once you sign up to the whole package, kids are also helped along by an on-screen cartoon assistant.

Zeeks http://www.zeeks.com Another American kids' portal, aimed at the older end of the 7–12 age group. If you pay a subscription, you get it ad-free.

....

Kids' downloads

....

Actually, you can download screensavers, wallpapers, software and on-screen toys from all sorts of sites. Just keep your eyes open for 'Download' or 'Free Stuff' sections when you're browsing. Here are a few of the specialist download sites.

Download.com **http://download.cnet.com/**. Huge site from the big net news operation C/Net. Look for the 'Home and Education' and 'Games' sections.

Family Games **http://www.familygames.com**. Loads of family-themed games and software, plus reviews and tips on downloading.

Kids Domain **http://www.kidsdomain.com/**. Excellent site with links to loads of free educational/entertainment programs, software for parents and general reviews.

Kids Freeware **http://www.kidsfreeware.com**. It does what it says on the tin – loads of links to free programs, plus parental advice.

Tucows **http://www.tucows.com**. Another big general download site – you should find some child-friendly stuff in the sections devoted to games and screensavers.

Special interest sites

Arts and crafts

One thing to look out for with sites in this section – the American ones use the American spelling of 'color' in their web addresses, which might trip you up if you're not careful.

Art for Kids http://artforkids.about.com. Superb set of links covering all sorts of arts and crafts information – learn about art around the world or discover how to make your own play-dough and slime.

The @rt Room http://www.arts.ufl.edu/art/rt_room/. Loads of material intended to stimulate kids' creativity – from 'artist scrabble' to learning how to think like an artist.

Art Safari http://artsafari.moma.org. An interesting online game that draws kids into making up stories about some of the artworks at the US Museum of Modern Art.

Aunt Annie's Crafts http://www.auntannie.com/. Suitably home-y and very popular page devoted to crafts of all kinds, from creating your own puppets to making paper flowers.

Cartoon Critters http://www.cartooncritters.com/. Tips on how to draw, mazes to print out, colouring books, jigsaw puzzles and more at the cheerful site.

Chunky Monkey http://www.chunkymonkey.com/. A page about a cartoon you may not know – but it has some good tips for kids who want to draw their own cartoons.

Color Matters http://www.colormatters.com/entercolormatters.html. Useful site for older kids beginning to think more about art – lots of info here about colour and its effects.

Coloring4Kids http://www.coloringpage.org/. Another excellent colouring sites with all sorts of images to colour, plus some useful links to other sites.

Dave Pilkey's Website of Fun http://www.pilkey.com. Bright and breezy site from a professional author/illustrator with drawing tips and loads of things to print out and play with.

Funorama http://www.funorama.com. Get directions for making mobiles and paper dolls or learn how to draw cowboys at this accessible site.

Haring Kids http://www.haringkids.com/. Excellent set of activities, online games and lesson plans themed around the graffiti art of the late Keith Haring.

Kaleidoscope Painter http://www.permadi.com/java/spaint/spaint.html. Amusing online tool which lets you click your mouse and create a kind of interactive kaleidoscope.

Kids Domain Craft Exchange http://www.kidsdomain.com/craft/. Excellent craft portal, which has tips on creating gifts, seasonal crafts, recycling and much more.

Kidzart http://www.kidzart.org. Another site designed to showcase kids' art from around the world, this also has advice about computer art and school projects.

Liana's Paper Dolls http://www-personal.umich.edu/~lsharer/paperdolls/. This is packed with loads of different dolls you can print and cut out. Liana isn't updating the site any more but it's still worth a visit.

Pieces and Creases http://tqjunior.thinkquest.org/5402/. There are loads of sites about paper folding and origami – this is one of the better efforts.

Professor Wonder http://www.professorwonder.com/balloon.htm. Tips on how to make balloon animals from the self-styled Professor Wonder.

Books and comics

If your child has a favourite author or illustrator, it's likely that they'll find something about them online – either an official site put up by the artist or their publishers or a fan site, many of which are excellent. Look in one of the kids' directories for links to author pages.

Beano Town http://www.beano.co.uk. The honorary online home of Dennis the Menace and the rest of the gang – join a club, find out about the comic's past or just browse.

Dorling Kindersley http://www.dk.com/uk/. From the publisher of big glossy kids' books, this site features a kids' encyclopedia, advice on surfing the net and creating your own website, plus links to kids' sites from around the world.

Harry Potter http://www.bloomsburymagazine.com/harrypotter/. There are countless sites devoted to J.K. Rowling's young wizard – this is the official one from the British publisher. There's one site for wizards and another for Muggles here.

The History of Batman http://www.dccomics.com/features/bmtch/bchmain.htm. Lots of info here about the Dark Knight, from DC Comics, who should know.

Just For Kids Who Love Books http://www.alanbrown.com. Vast collection of links to favourite kids' books and authors, plus reviews written by kids.

KidNews http://www.kidnews.com. Well-designed site that showcases news reports, stories and poems written by kids from around the world. Your kids can send in their own news too if they like.

KidsReads http://www.kidsreads.com/index.asp. Hosted by Booker T. Worm, this is basically a rather good webzine about kids' books, with features, reviews and lots of extras – trivia quizzes, word searches and the like.

Kid's Story http://www.kidstory.com/. Read stories written by kids, then get yours to send in their own. They can also send in illustrations, if they like.

Marvel Comics http://www.marvelcomics.com/. The official online home of Spiderman, The X-Men and many more – get news, previews and more here.

Narnia http://www.narnia.com. The official website for C.S. Lewis's Narnia stories. Read excerpts here and find out much more about the world he created and the people and creatures that live there.

The Neverending Tale http://www.coder.com/creations/tale/. An online 'choose-your-own-path adventure story', this serves up stories for your kids to read, add to and change, in collaboration with other kids.

Roald Dahl http://www.roalddahl.com. Brilliantly animated site devoted to the much-loved author – this has Quentin Blake's illustrations, lots of information about Dahl and some amusing games.

Scholastic http://www.scholastic.com/kids/index.htm. A worthwhile site from the US kids' publisher, this has stuff on *Harry Potter*, *Animorphs*, *Goosebumps* and many more well-known titles.

Seussville http://www.randomhouse.com/seussville/. One for the younger kids – a suitably charming site devoted to *The Cat in the Hat* and the rest of Dr Seuss's menagerie, with games, contests and lots of dodgy rhymes.

StoryPlace http://www.storyplace.org/. Created by another group of American librarians, this is meant to be the online equivalent of a public library – it has reviews and reading lists, a pre-school section and games and interactive stories.

TinTin http://www.tintin.com/uk/. A very swish site devoted to the comic-book character much loved by mums and dads (and kids).

**Write Me A Story
http://www.kidscom.com/orakc/Write/writestoryright.html**. Kids are challenged to write a story incorporating elements suggested by the site. Five are then selected at random, and kids read them and vote for a winner.

Collecting, hobbies and pets

Collecting Kids' Toys **http://kidscollecting.about.com/index.htm**.
About.com's collecting site is perhaps as much for adults as kids, but
there's loads of useful links here.

Conjuror – Free Magic Tricks **http://conjuror.com/magictricks/**.
Directions for fifteen tricks (the self-tying handkerchief, for instance) that
are apparently suitable for the young magician.

Everything Animals **http://www.everythinganimals.co.uk/**. A British pet
portal that has animal news and tips on keeping a variety of pets, from
cats and dogs to reptiles and horses.

Hocus Pocus Palace **http://www.teleport.com/~jrolsen/index.shtml**.
Home of the Great Mysto, this site offers magic that works over the net
and loads of links to magic resources online.

The British House Rabbit Society **http://www.houserabbit.co.uk/**. The
website of Britain's leading association for rabbit-lovers has loads of
information and advice for on looking after pet bunnies.

Guinea Pig Compendium
http://www.aracnet.com/~seagull/Guineas/#Care. Another useful pet
resource, this site claims to be the most comprehensive resource of
guinea pig information on the net. Hard to disagree.

Kids' Gardening **http://www.kidsgardening.com/**. Children can pick up all
sorts of gardening tips at this American site. Start them early and you'll
have them mowing the lawn in no time.

My First Garden **http://www.urbanext.uiuc.edu/firstgarden/**. Very child-
friendly gardening site, with lots of age-appropriate projects and advice.

Net Pets **http://www.chirpingbird.com/netpets/html/main/intro.html**.
Your kids will find lots of pet-related fun and general animal info at this
engagingly cartoony site.

Pet Health Council **http://www.pethealthcouncil.co.uk**. Look in the People
and Pets section for advice on getting and looking after a pet. There are
also lots of contact details for UK pet organizations.

Pet Website http://www.petwebsite.com/. A clearly designed pet portal, with news and discussion boards, along with the usual advice on looking after furry friends.

The Pony Club http://www.pony-club.org.uk. Find out where your local branch of the Pony Club is and get advice about buying and looking after a pony.

RSPCA Online http://www.rspca.org.uk/. Kids and grown-ups should find this site useful. The Kids section has a cyberpet you can look after, plus general animal facts. Elsewhere you'll find specific advice for pet owners.

Smithsonian Kids – Collecting http://kids.si.edu/collecting/main.html. The well-known US museum's mini-site about collecting, this has tips on coins, stamps and rocks and fossils, plus stories about some amazing collections.

Simple Magik http://www.angelfire.com/pe/SimpleMagik/. Yet more how-to advice, covering tricks like 'coins from the air' and 'balls from nowhere'.

Stamp Collecting For Kids http://www.bnaps.org/stamps4kids/. Loads of information about stamp collecting for younger kids and teens, from tips about getting started to advice on condition and value.

Trains.com http://www.trains.com/home.asp. Not a full-blown trainspotter site, but it's getting close – this American site is for everyone who loves trains, both the real thing and the model variety.

Films, TV and cartoons

Most TV shows for kids now come with websites where they can get all sorts of extras designed to build loyalty and get them to tune in next week. Look out for web addresses at the end of the shows they like. Similarly, big kids' films usually have big promotional websites where you can watch trailers and play games. Look out for web addresses on the posters and promotional material. Finally, some of the online cartoon sites are aimed more at the 16–25 age-group and aren't really suitable for younger kids.

Aardman **http://www.aardman.com/**. The online home of the people behind *Wallace and Gromit* and *Chicken Run*. Some of their content – *Angry Kid* and *Rex the Runt* – is aimed at older kids/adults, so take care.

AOL KidsWB **http://aol.kidswb.com/**. You'll find information and extras relating to Warner Bros' various kid-related films and cartoons here.

The Cartoon Factory **http://www.cartoon-factory.com/**. This site is probably aimed more at grown-ups who collect memorabilia associated with classic cartoons, but you'll find some good introductory info about how they're made here too.

Cartoon Network **http://www.cartoonnetwork.com**. Another huge TV-based site – you'll find games and online cartoons, alongside pages for the channel's big names (Scooby Doo, Batman, Bugs Bunny...).

Cartoon World **http://www.cet.com/~rascal/welcome.html**. Great site with information about all kinds of cartoons, from big names like Disney and Warner Bros to less familiar titles.

CBBC **http://www.bbc.co.uk/cbbc/**. Quizzes, competitions, message boards and links to the mini-sites for various well-known BBC kids' shows, like *Blue Peter* and *Grange Hill*.

CITV **http://www.citv.co.uk**. ITV's portal for its various kids' shows, this has all the usual features – games, polls, special mini-sites and so on.

Disney http://disney.go.com/. Resistance is futile, as all parents know. The main Disney site has links to sections for kids, pre-schoolers and loads of general info about the films/videos.

How are Hollywood films made?
http://www.learner.org/exhibits/cinema/. An illuminating step-by-step guide to making films, from scripts to editing, plus some useful links.

Kids' Corner http://www.media-awareness.ca/eng/med/kids/kindex.htm. A site that uses games and stories to help kids become more media/net literate. Worthwhile.

Nick http://www.nick.com. A kids' portal from Nickelodeon. This has the usual stuff – games, message boards, cartoons and so on – plus special sites devoted to the channel's big shows.

The Museum of Television http://www.mztv.com/mztvhome.html. Find out about the history of the goggle box at this online companion to a real world Canadian museum.

Nova Online http://www.pbs.org/wgbh/nova/specialfx/sfxhome.html. Find out more about film special effects – what they can do, and how they do it, from this interesting TV spin-off site.

PBS Kids http://pbskids.org/. The US home of the kind of kids' show parents love (apart from *Barney*, perhaps). You'll find pages about the big purple dinosaur, *Arthur* and more here.

Pixar http://www.pixar.com/. Online home of the company behind *Toy Story*, *A Bug's Life* and more. In the 'Fun Stuff' section, you'll find some info on how they do it.

Rugrats http://www.cooltoons.com/shows/rugrats/home.html. This *Rugrats* site was put up by Klaszky Csupo, the company behind the show. Loads of interesting stuff – plus, if you go back to Cooltoons.com you'll find information about their other shows, for example *The Wild Thornberries*.

The Simpsons http://www.thesimpsons.com. The official site, this is one for older kids (and their parents) – lots of basic information about the shows, but not that many fun extras.

SM:tv **http://www.smtvlive.co.uk/smtv/**. The Saturday morning show the kids (and sad students) prefer. Play Wonkey Donkey online, come up with your own plot for *Chums* and more.

Star Wars **http://www.starwars.com/**. The net is packed with *Star Wars* fan sites. It's probably best for kids to start with this official effort.

Thunderbirds **http://www.thunderbirdsonline.com**. One for the dads. Get 'craft profiles' of the various Thunderbirds, plus lots of information and downloads.

Food and drink

Many of the big fizzy drinks / sweets / cereals brands now put up websites devoted to their products. These sites usually have more positive effects on brains than some of the products do on teeth, so they can be worth a visit. Again, look out for web addresses on adverts and promotional material.

The Apple A Day **http://www.theappleaday.co.uk**. Lots of information here aimed at teaching kids to eat healthily and generally look after themselves.

BugFood **http://www.uky.edu/Agriculture/Entomology/ythfacts/ bugfood/bugfood.htm**. Part of the University of Kentucky's Entomology Department's site for kids, this has information about insect-themed food (cakes that look like bugs) and insects as food…which is a bit different.

CadburyLand **http://www.cadbury-land.co.uk**. A flashy, kid-friendly site from the big British chocolate manufacturer, this has games, chocolate recipes, puzzles and competitions.

The Chocolate Lovers' Page **http://www.chocolocate.com/**. It's a rather confusing web address, but it makes sense, sort of. A page of links to pretty much every chocolate-related page on the web.

The International Children's Cookbook **http://www.b.shuttle.de/museum/kochbuch.htm**. A collection of recipes submitted by kids from around the world – look for the English version at the bottom of the page.

Kids' Health **http://kidshealth.org**. Very useful site designed to teach kids about their bodies and minds and how to keep both in good working order.

Kids' Kitchen **http://www.scoreone.com/kids_kitchen/**. A great kids-driven recipe site where you'll find tips on making major messes, sweets and munchies, along with a recipe competition.

Pancake http://www.sirius.com/~pancake/welcome.html. A site devoted to all things to do with pancakes. Apart from standard recipes, the Kids section has super-sweet variations your offspring will probably love.

Popcorn http://www.popcorn.org/index.cfm. Find out about the history of popcorn and its nutritional value (really?) and play a few games at this slick site.

The Wild World of Wonka http://www.wonka.com. Shouldn't this be in the section devoted to books or films? Actually, it's here because it's been put together by Nestlé to plug its Wonka sweets. Still fun, though.

Fun and games

Most of the big toy brands have companion websites, most of which are worth a visit. Of course, the toy market is more fad driven than most. If your kids are still into Pokémon/Digimon, it's pretty easy to find the relevant sites via a kids' directory. If they're into something newer, like Rumble Robots, they're also easy to track down.

Action Man **http://www.actionman.com**. The online home of the well-known boys' toy, this has online games, things to download and lots more.

Barbie **http://www.barbie.com**. The *über*-blonde's home on the web, this well-designed site has sections on music, fashion, ballet and more.

FunBrain **http://www.funbrain.com/**. Loads of colourful games and quizzes for kids of all ages, plus a few tests for parents to do.

FunPlanet **http://www.funplanet.co.uk**. An online games portal, where your kids will find loads of ways to waste time, from traditional card games to arcade games.

Games Domain **http://www.gamesdomain.co.uk**. One of the best video/computer games sites, this has news, reviews, tips and cheats on just about every game going.

JokeZone **http://www.owl.on.ca/owl/joke.html**. Your kids can find riddles, knock-knock jokes and more to torment you with at this engaging site.

Kids' Jokes **http://www.kidsjokes.co.uk**. A British repository of kids' gags, this has monster jokes, school jokes, 'doctor doctor' jokes, tongue twisters and more.

Lego **http://www.lego.com**. The ultimate construction toy's home on the web doesn't disappoint – loads of games that will please you as much as your kids. Look out for the Lego Mosaic feature.

Mensa Workout **http://www.mensa.org/workout.html**. There are loads of quizzes online – this one looks like one of the more hardcore efforts.

104 Knock-Knock Jokes **http://www.azkidsnet.com/JSknockjoke.htm**.
Gives you exactly what it says. Plus you'll find brainteasers, riddles and
assorted silly questions. And your kids can send in their own jokes.

Robot Gallery **http://www.chaoskids.com/ROBOTS/directory.html**.
Possibly more for dads than their kids – an online gallery of toy robots,
with details about when they were made.

The Sims **http://www.thesims.com**. The web companion to one of the best
computer games of recent years. If your kids like the game, they'll find all
sorts of extras here to download.

Thunk **http://www.thunk.com**. A fun online tool that lets kids send each
other secret scrambled messages.

Toys Were Us **http://www.discovery.com/stories/history/toys/toys.html**.
A Discovery Channel mini-site devoted to the history of toys, this has
special features on Barbie, skateboarding and Frisbees.

Yahooligans Games **http://games.yahoo.com/games/yahooligans.html**.
The kids' directory's special games zone has online versions of board
games, card games and more.

Wooden Toy Museum **http://www.woodentoymuseum.com/index.htm**.
Your kids can check out some very old toys alongside some newer
wooden playthings here.

....

History

....

One great way to find out about history online is via the sites put up by museums. There are museums dotted throughout the sections in this directory. But if you're looking for a central site where you can find out about the UK's various museums, try the excellent 24hour Museum **http://www.24hourmuseum.org.uk**.

A-Z History
http://school.discovery.com/homeworkhelp/worldbook/atozhistory/.
The Discovery Channel's History Encyclopedia – click through to find articles on everything from the Battle of Actium to the Mexican revolutionary Emiliano Zapata.

BBC Modern World History http://www.bbc.co.uk/education/modern/.
A guide to twentieth century history aimed at GCSE students, this has articles on the key events and personalities, tests you can take and more.

British History http://britannia.com/history/. An impressively comprehensive site devoted to British history, this features timelines, links to source documents, key texts and lots more.

EyeWitness http://www.ibiscom.com/. History through the eyes of those who lived it – which means first-person accounts of different periods, from the ancient world up to the twentieth century.

The History Channel http://www.historychannel.com. The online extension of the History Channel, this has a great regular feature on what happened on 'this day in history', among other things.

History Learning Site http://www.historylearningsite.co.uk/. Low tech site – it's mainly just text and links, but loads of good historical information for kids from 7–16 and beyond.

Hyper History Online
http://www.hyperhistory.com/online_n2/History_n2/a.html. A series of clickable timelines and graphic maps that let kids explore history intuitively – they can track famous people through history, or look at the rise and fall of different civilizations.

You Be The Historian
http://americanhistory.si.edu/hohr/springer/index.htm. Engaging
interactive site that aims to get kids sifting evidence, looking for clues
and thinking like historians.

Homework and study

There are loads of websites that set out to support the work your kids do at school and help them with the work they bring home. Most of these are responsible outfits, often run by teachers and educational professionals. However, you should look out for older kids trying out some of the so-called 'paper mills' – things like schoolsucks.com. These are more popular in the States than here and are aimed more at college/university students, but your kids may be tempted. Some supply pre-prepared essays and term papers, many of which aren't that good. And increasingly teachers can spot this kind of computer-assisted plagiarism. The students who try it get into trouble. So keep an eye out for your older kids.

ArgoSphere http://www.argosphere.co.uk. An all-purpose UK educational site, with homework help, crosswords, quizzes and more.

BBC Education www.bbc.co.uk/education. The BBC's Education site has loads of resources kids can use to back up their schoolwork, plus revision sections for the various exams and tests.

GCSE Answers http://www.gcse.com/. Tutorials and advice on how to get your GCSEs in Maths, English, French and Physics.

Homework Elephant http://www.homeworkelephant.co.uk/. You'll find interactive web lessons, experts on hand to answer queries and general information about different subjects at this quality homework helper site.

Homework High http://www.4learning.co.uk/apps/homework/index.jsp. Got a question about your homework? Drop a line to this Channel 4 site and their team of experts should get back to you with helpful suggestions within a day. For under-16s.

Kevin's Playroom http://www.kevinsplayroom.co.uk/. An award-winning site that offers homework/school support to kids of all ages, from pre-school to secondary.

Learn.co.uk http://www.learn.co.uk. One of the *Guardian*'s own sites. There's loads of information designed to help kids and support the National Curriculum, plus some interesting projects – an online novel and a kids' fiction prize, for instance.

Project A Level http://www.projectalevel.co.uk. Revision guides, advice and more for older kids doing their AS/A2 levels.

Revise It http://www.revise.it. Tips on GCSEs and A-Levels, essay plans and advice on applying for university at this student-friendly site.

S-cool http://www.s-cool.co.uk. Useful site aimed at older kids doing GCSEs and A-Levels. You'll also find tips on writing CVs and advice on getting into university.

Schoolsnet http://www.schoolsnet.com. Huge portal aimed at pupils, parents and teachers. There's some useful advice on learning in the sections on lessons and revision.

Top Marks http://www.topmarks.co.uk. Huge UK-based educational portal with links to all sorts of kids' educational sites, plus special sections for parents and teachers.

Music

This section could have been filled with details on the websites of popular kid-friendly bands, from Britney to Westlife. However, by the time you read these, A1, S Club 7, Steps and the rest may have been put out to pasture and your kids might be on to new names. Most new boy/girl bands have their own websites – the best thing is to look for them yourself, either via a kids' directory or a filtered search engine. If you don't use the latter, you may find yourself accessing something rather inappropriate, especially if you search for sites relating to Britney Spears and other young female stars.

About.com Music for Teens http://teenmusic.about.com/. A vast selection of reviews, news and links, all of which should appeal to music-loving teens.

AllMusic http://www.allmusic.com. A massive music database where you'll find information and useful links relating to just about any musician/band you'd care to mention.

Artist Direct http://artistdirect.com. An excellent online music resource that comes in handy if you want to find fan sites and official sites devoted to your favourite artists.

Classical is Cool http://www.classicaliscool.com. Let's be honest, it's an embarrassing name, but the site is rather good. Download free music files, listen to online radio, get a quick classical 'moodfix' and more here.

Dot Music http://www.dotmusic.co.uk. A music news resource much used by industry types, but accessible to ordinary punters too.

Essentials of Music http://www.essentialsofmusic.com/main.html. A web-based classical music encyclopedia, this has sections on composers and eras and loads of sound samples.

Listen.com http://www.listen.com. An online music portal, this has sections on online radio stations, streaming pop videos and music files for download.

Lyrics World http://www.lyricsworld.com. Can't quite figure out the words to that song? Check in here and you might find some joy.

MTV http://www.mtv.com. Watch videos (obviously), hear new albums, share thoughts with other fans and more at this comprehensive site from the big music channel. One for teens.

Music Notes http://library.thinkquest.org/15413/. Your kids can learn about classical music history and theory here and play a few music-themed games too.

NME http://www.nme.com. One for older teenagers just beginning to take their music (too) seriously – and their Hornby-esque dads. Come here for news, reviews, links to music downloads and more.

Radio 1 http://www.bbc.co.uk/radio1. Again, one for older kids, who, apart from checking out the charts and Radio One playlist here, can also find out more about indie rock, R&B, dance and so on, watch videos, download free music and more.

PlayMusic http://www.playmusic.org. Engagingly animated site that aims to educate kids about orchestras and classical music.

Top of the Pops http://www.totp.beeb.com. Reviews, competitions and other content spun off from the Beeb's long running chart show.

Turntables http://www.turntables.de. An online music toy that lets you scratch like a real DJ – sort of. Lots of fun.

Nature

BBC Online – Animals http://www.bbc.co.uk/nature/animals/. A typically excellent online resource from the Beeb, this has information, links to webcams and more. Be sure to check out the mini-sites for *The Really Wild Show* and *Blue Planet*.

Animal Planet http://animal.discovery.com/. The Discovery Channel's special animal site, this has news stories, live cams and mini-sites based on the big shows.

Creature Feature http://www.nationalgeographic.com/kids/creature_ feature/0109/lions.html. A regular feature from National Geographic Online, this lets kids check facts and watch videos about different animals.

Dino-Roar http://www.sciam.com/explorations/121597dinosaur/. What did the dinosaurs sound like? The site from *Scientific American* has a few answers and some sound files to download.

Dinosauria http://www.dinosauria.com. A dinosaur database on the web, this lets your kids catch up on the latest dino-research and check names and terms in a dinosaur omnipedia.

EcoKids Online http://ecokids.earthday.ca. One of the many sites online devoted to educating kids about green issues, this 'online tree-house' is worth a click or two.

Eden Project http://www.edenproject.com. Home of the much-praised Cornish bio-domes on the net, this has useful information if you're going to visit, plus games and quizzes. Your kids should also look at the *Guardian*'s own Eden Project site at **http://www.learn.co.uk/edenproject**.

ExZooBerance http://www.exzooberance.com/. As you may have gathered from the name, this site sets out be a 'virtual zoo' and has photo galleries, news and links to animal webcams.

Kids Go Wild http://www.kidsgowild.com. The Wildlife Conservation Society's site for kids, this has animal facts and pics, plus conservation advice.

Natural History Museum http://www.nhm.ac.uk. An excellent site from the well-known London museum, this has details on current real-world exhibits plus loads of online interactive routines and 'learning journeys'.

Nature Serve http://www.natureserve.org/. A seriously useful resource, this 'online encyclopedia of life' has detailed conservation information about plants, animals and ecological communities.

Secrets at Sea http://www.secretsatsea.org. An amusing online mystery game, this aims to teach kids about the oceans of the world. Nicely designed.

Walking with Dinosaurs http://www.bbc.co.uk/dinosaurs/. The BBC's companion to its much-praised show, this has loads of dino-data, downloads and games.

The Weird Animal Express http://tqjunior.thinkquest.org/5801/. An accessible site aimed at younger children, this has information on some of the more unusual animals in the world.

What is it like where you live? http://mbgnet.mobot.org/index.htm. Learn about the world's different ecosystems at this colourful site.

Reference

Britannica **http://www.britannica.com**. The online extension of the Encyclopedia Britannica – a superb collection of facts and articles and more.

Encarta **http://www.encarta.msn.com**. The online companion of Microsoft's CD-ROM encyclopedia – lots of links, quizzes and other extras.

Guinness World Records **http://www.guinnessrecords.com/**. One of those reference sources kids love – find out about the latest world records here.

Research It **http://www.itools.com/research-it**. A page of links to dictionaries, thesauri, maps, currency converters and more.

World Flag Database **http://www.flags.ndirect.co.uk/mainindex.htm**. Find out which country has which flag, learn about the history of flags and more here.

Xrefer **http://www.xrefer.com**. This trimmed down no-nonsense site offers free access to over 50 different research databases online – better for older kids.

Science

Brain Pop **http://www.brainpop.com**. Online cartoons and activity pages designed to teach kids about science, technology and health.

Cool Math **http://www.coolmath.com**. An online maths amusement park, apparently – which means loads of games and puzzles involving primary school maths. Lots of fun.

The Exploratorium **http://www.exploratorium.edu**. Online companion to a much-praised museum of 'science, art and human perception' in San Francisco – a good place to start is the Learning Studio.

How Things Work **http://howthingswork.virginia.edu**. Text-heavy but very illuminating site from Professor Louis A. Bloomfield, who will answer your queries about the physics of everyday life.

Learn2 Everyday **http://www.learn2.com/learn2_everyday.asp**. A selection of tutorials designed to teach you and your kids how to do everything from making a paper hat to writing a thank-you note.

Learning Planet **http://www.learningplanet.com/**. Lots of web-based educational games covering both art and science – the Math Mayhem section is worth a click.

Mad Science for Kids **http://www.madscience.org/entrance/Kids/index.htm**. Experiments to do at home and cool science facts to bamboozle parents at this accessible and perky site.

Maths with Alice **http://library.thinkquest.org/10977/main.html**. The two cultures collide productively in this site that uses Lewis Carroll's *Alice* stories to teach kids about maths.

Nasa Kids **http://kids.msfc.nasa.gov/**. The US Space Agency's home on the web for kids. Find out about rockets, astronauts and space and play a few educational games about gravity and the like.

The Science Museum **http://www.sciencemuseum.org.uk/**. Online home of the Science Museum – look in the Learn and Teach section for lots of kid-friendly content.

The Tech Museum of Innovation
http://www.thetech.org/section-discover.html. Online home of the California Museum of Innovation, this hosts a Robot Zoo, a PC Webopedia and interviews with the people behind the computer revolution.

Try Science http://www.tryscience.org/home.html. A site that aims to get kids excited about contemporary science, this has suggestions for experiments, online interactive exhibits and links to science-based webcams.

Ultimate Computer Source http://library.thinkquest.org/25018/. The name gets it about right – loads of information here about the history of computing, programming, a computer jargon glossary and more.

A Virtual Journey into the Universe
http://library.thinkquest.org/28327/. Flash-enhanced site that takes kids on a simulated space cruise and teaches them a bit about astronomy on the way.

Wizzkidz http://www.wizzkidz.com. Cheerful and friendly site packed with educational games covering maths, science and English. Probably best for younger kids.

Sport

Many of the big sports teams, especially Premiership football clubs now have their own websites. This section could have been filled with URLs for Manchester United, Liverpool, Arsenal and the rest. It seemed like a better idea to highlight a few other things. But if you want to find the site for your child's favourite team, have a look in a good kids' directory or try a filtered search engine.

BBC Sport **http://www.bbc.co.uk/sport/**. They may not have as much sport as they used to, but the Beeb's site is as dependable as ever – stats, reports and opinion on just about everything.

Board World **http://library.thinkquest.org/J002968/**. Rather minimal but nevertheless informative, this site has information about skateboarding stars, styles and tricks.

Cric Info **http://www.cricket.org**. Comprehensive site that covers cricket around the world, with news, reports on current matches, a stats database and some interactive games.

Formula 1 **http://www.formula-1.com**. Not the official Formula One site, but one of the best – catch the latest news and gossip, read up on the history and chat to other fans.

Icons **http://www.icons.com**. The place where all the big-name footballers from the Premiership and beyond have their own homepages.

Jump Into Snowboarding **http://tqjunior.thinkquest.org/3885/**. A useful introduction to snowboarding, this site cover the sport's history, its arrival in the Olympics and the big question – are you goofy or regular?

KidzUnited **http://www.kidzunited.com**. A very engaging site about football aimed specifically at kids, this has competitions, coaching tips, news and much more.

Kids Running **http://www.kidsrunning.com/**. A site for kids who are serious about running, from *Runner's World Magazine*, this has training plans, news about fun runs and advice for schools.

NBA **http://www.nba.com**. Home of America's National Basketball Association, this has news and views about all the big names and their teams.

Planet Football **http://www.planetfootball.com**. Wide-ranging site that majors on the Premiership, but has news and results from football across Europe and around the world.

Rollerblade.com **http://www.rollerblade.com**. The official home of rollerblading on the web, this has advice on getting started, tips on gear and information on skating for fitness.

Sport For Kids **http://members.aol.com/msdaizy/sports/locker.html**. Low tech but still excellent site that offers no-nonsense coaching advice for a variety of sports, from basketball and swimming to tennis and volleyball.

Sports Illustrated for Kids **http://www.sikids.com/index.html**. The kids' edition of the well-known American sports magazine, this has a transatlantic focus, obviously, but is still worth a look.

Sport Science **http://www.exploratorium.edu/sports/index.html**. Learn about the science behind skateboarding, cycling, hockey and baseball at one of the Exploratorium's various mini-sites.

WWF **http://www.wwf.com**. Is wrestling a sport or is it really some sort of meathead ballet? Your kids don't care either way, but they'll probably thank you for pointing them towards this site.

Teenagers

As kids get older, they'll be more than happy to pick out their own sites. They won't need or want your advice. That said, here are a few sites that might help them out. Most of the following are aimed at 12–16 year-olds, but two or three are suitable for older teenagers.

About.com Teen Advice **http://teenadvice.about.com/**. Teenagers facing problems should find useful links and help here.

Cyberteens **http://www.cyberteens.com/**. Worthwhile online hang-out for older teenagers – they can chat, swap ideas, send in art and stories and more.

So **http://www.bbc.co.uk/so/**. The BBC's webzine for teenagers, this has horoscopes, pop gossip, quizzes, chatrooms and an agony aunt.

Teenhoopla **http://www.ala.org/teenhoopla/links.html**. The American Library Association's page of links to teenage sites on the web – very useful.

Google Teen Life
http://directory.google.com/Top/Kids_and_Teens/Teen_Life/. The teenage section in Google's web directory has loads of links to teen-friendly sites – definitely worth a visit.

Life Bytes **http://www.lifebytes.gov.uk/**. A snappily presented health advice site aimed at 11–14 year-olds, this covers relationships, alcohol, drugs and healthy eating, among other things.

Radio 1 Essentials **http://www.bbc.co.uk/radio1/essentials/**. Another BBC site – this has loads of advice about money, studying, work and travel – aimed more at older teens and students.

Teenage girls

There are lots of portals for teenage/tweenage girls online. They're mostly like an online version of a girls' magazine and as such are pretty harmless. However, keep an eye out for sites put up by market research companies, which use bright and breezy sites to do research in teens/tweens' likes and dislikes, and give them reward points for doing surveys and polls. There's nothing wrong with this so long as your kids (and you) know what they're getting into.

Generation Girl http://www.generationgirl.com. Site aimed at 8–12 year-old girls and backed by various doll manufacturers. The usual pop gossip, with murals and posters to download and print.

Girl Tech http://www.girltech.com/home.html. A general site devoted to girls who like messing around with technology and computers, this has info about women inventors, discussion boards and lots of links to other 'girl' sites.

A Girl's World http://www.agirlsworld.com. A clearly designed portal for 'girls and teens', this has chat, pen pals, diaries, advice and more.

A Girl Like U http://www.agirllikeu.com. Teen-friendly spelling and a teen-friendly site, with advice on money, school and hanging out. Do you really need advice on the latter?

My Kinda Place http://www.mykindaplace.com/. A British rival of the American teen girl sites, this has the usual content – pop gossip, polls, chats and discussion – wrapped in a less cheesy design than usual.

Toddlers

AllKids http://www.allkids.co.uk. A sort of pre-school portal, with special
sections devoted to kids aged one, two, three and four. Each section
features colouring, counting games, rhymes and the like. Very useful.

**Enchanted Learning
http://www.enchantedlearning.com/categories/preschool.shtml**. The
special pre-school area on this excellent site – you'll find letter print-outs,
colouring books, games and more here.

The Idea Box http://www.theideabox.com/. Very American-oriented site,
but still fine for all that, with lots of suggestions about activities and
games for the pre-school set.

Little Explorers http://www.littleexplorers.com. Super online picture
dictionary from Enchanted Learning that lets kids find out about words
and learn the basics of surfing.

Little Kids http://www.bbc.co.uk/littlekids. The BBC's general site for
its various pre-school shows, from *Noddy* to *The Tweenies* – download
pictures to colour in, songs to sing along to, read stories and send
e-cards.

Nick Jr http://www.nickjr.com. Nickelodeon's pre-school site, with info
about shows like *Blue's Clues*, various 'printables' (things to colour) and
tips for parents.

Sesame Workshop http://www.sesameworkshop.org/. You'll find loads of
little games and interactive learning routines here, using the characters
from *Sesame Street*.

Small Films http://www.smallfilms.co.uk/. The website for the company
set up by Oliver Postgate and Peter Firmin, the people behind *Bagpuss*,
The Clangers, *Noggin the Nog* and more. You'll find links here to sites
devoted to all their big shows.

Rebus Rhymes http://www.enchantedlearning.com/Rhymes.html.
Another Enchanted Learning site, this time about nursery rhymes – lots of
excellent content here, as usual.

Disney's Playhouse **http://disney.go.com/**. Click the Playhouse link on the main Disney page and you go to the online home of *Winnie the Pooh* and their other pre-school product.

Weird, scary and yucky

As they get older, some kids will be drawn to some of the weirder/scarier sites online. They will also probably try to look at some of the sites specializing in gross pictures. Try to keep them away from Rotten.com, which is really not suitable for kids. The gross sites in this section are better. Obviously, the sites in this section are really only for older kids.

Aliens: Worlds of Possibility
http://exhibits.pacsci.org/aliens/welcome2.html. One of the more level-headed alien sites online, this takes a scientific look at the chances of life out there somewhere.

The Belch Page **http://www.goobo.com/belch/index.html**. You know your kids will love it – download various disgusting belch noises here.

Dracula's Homepage **http://www.ucs.mun.ca/~emiller/**. Not for younger kids, obviously. This sites hosts a variety of material connected with both vampires and Bram Stoker's original novel.

Fortean Picture Archive **http://www.forteanpix.demon.co.uk/main.html**. A collection of pictures of strange things – UFOs, ghosts, fairies, yetis and such like. Again, one for older kids.

Gareth Long's Encyclopedia of Monsters
http://webhome.idirect.com/~donlong/monsters/frmain.htm. Not sure who Gareth is, but his database of strange beasts and mythical creatures is definitely fun to browse.

GhostWeb **http://www.ghostweb.com**. The online home of the International Ghost Hunters Society, this has 'educational articles', pictures and creepy 'true stories'.

The Museum of Unnatural Mystery
http://www.unmuseum.mus.pa.us/unmuseum.htm. A sort of all-purpose online museum of weird and mysterious stuff, from UFOs to living dinosaurs like Nessie.

PsiTest **http://www.geocities.com/Area51/Zone/2788/**. Do you think you might be pychic? Take a test here and find out how gullible you are.

Shadowlands **http://theshadowlands.net/ghost/**. A place where people can share 'true ghost stories', get help in dealing with them, or just scare each other slightly. Fun, but not for younger kids.

This Spectred Isle **http://freespace.virgin.net/martin.lightburn.** This 'gazetteer of British ghosts' tells you which spooks are haunting which bits of the UK.

Strange But True **http://www.strangefacts.com**. An amusing list of offbeat facts ('it's against the law to pawn your dentures in Las Vegas', for instance) that your kids can torment you with.

UFO Info **http://www.ufoinfo.com**. If your kids want to dig into the whole UFO culture, this site, which has loads of information but avoids UFO-based religious cults, is probably the best place to start.

The Yuckiest Site on the Net **http://yucky.kids.discovery.com/**. The acceptable way for kids to gross out – this Discovery Channel site has the lowdown on worms, roaches, belching, farting, zits, earwax and more.

5

Protecting your kids online

So much media attention has focused on the dodgier aspects of the net, that some parents, unsurprisingly, are convinced that their kids will be assaulted by pornographers and paedophiles as soon as they log on. Fortunately, that's not the case. There are paedophiles online, but not in the numbers claimed by some of the more alarmist media commentators. Similarly, there is plenty of porn online. But generally, with some exceptions, which were detailed earlier in the book, it doesn't jump out at you unbidden. You need to go looking for it.

That said, although would-be moral guardians do sometimes overstate the dangers of the net, you and your children do need to take care. Like the real world, there are people online who do not have your kids' best interests at heart. The net is such a new space that sometimes you might not realize that your kids are getting into trouble. But don't worry. There are a number of things you can do to keep your family safe online. You're already halfway there: you've read this book and begun to learn about the net and how it works. The next step is to get an accurate idea of the real problems your kids might face online and what you can do about them.

Your children's risks

Despite the impression given by some of the more simplistic coverage of the online world, the net is not one big undifferentiated entity. Different parts of the net carry different risks. Some areas (IRC chatrooms and Usenet newsgroups in particular) are more risky for children than others. I've tried to outline the specific problems associated with the web, email, chat and the rest in the relevant parts of Section 2. There are, however, a few general risks that should be highlighted:

- Your child might access information that is inappropriate, upsetting or dangerous. Most parents focus on porn, but they should also worry about hate/intolerance, gory/gross images, misinformation, crackpot conspiracy theories and sites that feature information that has the potential to lead to actual physical harm – e.g. bomb-making advice.

- Your child might be harassed whilst online by so-called 'cyberstalkers', who send them threatening emails and viruses, hack into their computers and worse.

- Your child might give away personal or private information that could then be used either by unscrupulous marketing types or people looking to get access to them in the real world.

- Your child might be targeted by 'cyberpredators', whose aim is to trick them into a meeting online. There aren't as many 'cyberpredators' out there as some in the media would have you believe. But there's evidence that those who are there are prepared to spend months cultivating relationships with their targets, in the hope of ultimately persuading them to meet up in the real world.

- If you allow your child access to a credit card, they might buy things online that are dangerous/illegal for them to possess. This is something that happens more in the States than here. That said, it is theoretically possible for children armed with a credit card to buy various forms of illegal material, from alcohol to medical drugs like Viagra, or to gamble online. So the thing to do is to make sure they don't gain access to your credit cards and the information they need to use them.

Some of these risks are obviously more serious than others. Things that stay on screen aren't as bad as things that spill over into the real world. Inappropriate information has the potential to upset children badly. But it won't cause them actual physical harm. However, there's a good chance this will happen if a child logs off and heads out into the real world to meet the 'cyberpredator' who has managed to convince them that he's their friend. So get things in perspective and act accordingly. Some advice on dealing with each of these problems follows shortly.

Your risks

Most parents focus on bad things that might happen to their kids whilst they're online. That's understandable. However, if they don't do the right thing on the net, your kids can end up causing problems for other people, including you. So what could they get up to?

- They might threaten or harass other users. Plenty of cyberstalking cases involve children, who use the power of the net and the superficial anonymity it confers to act out fantasies and generally throw their weight around.

- They might indulge in online pranks that could lead to the family net account being cancelled.

- By failing to take the proper precautions, they may infect the family computer with viruses.

- They might hack into computers belonging to other people and to companies or government agencies.

- They might say things online that lead to them (and you) being sued for libel.

- They might infringe copyright restrictions and, as a result, end up being sued.

- They might use your credit card details to buy things online without your knowledge. While trying to shop online, they might also be conned into giving away your credit card data to people who will misuse it.

Some of these problems are easier to deal with than others. If you make sure you don't leave your credit card details/net passwords lying around, then you make it a lot harder for your kids to go around buying stuff and charging it to you. Others are relatively uncommon. Very few children get into the kind of hardcore hacking that gets them into trouble with the authorities. So again, you need to prioritize these problems and take action accordingly. There are more specific tips coming up shortly.

Using work accounts at home Some parents use their workplace net accounts at home. If you do, it can cause real problems if you also let your child use this account. Workplace net use is not private. Most companies now use surveillance programs to track what their employees do online. They have strict rules about what's acceptable online. If your child breaks those while using the net at home, it could have serious repercussions for you at the office.

Minimizing the risks

Many parents think that they need to resort to technology, specifically internet filtering software, to protect their kids when they use the net. These programs, which essentially create barriers between your child and the online world, are useful. But they're not without problems. And before you resort to buying new bits of software, there are plenty of low tech measures you can take that may prove just as effective in the long run.

1. Put the family computer in a shared 'family' space.

If you do this, the computer becomes something that belongs to you as well as your kids. You can keep an eye on them as they use the net. And even when you're not in the room, there's always the possibility you will walk in, which may stop them from getting up to things. This is a good basic measure but you need to follow it up in various ways:

- Don't let your child password-protect areas of the computer.

- Learn how to use the computer yourself. Make it yours as well as theirs. Use it regularly and check any new programs that appear on it.

- Don't leave your important personal information lying around near or on the computer. In particular, don't put your ISP account password or your credit card details in an easy-to-access file on the computer. Don't put temptation in your child's way.

As kids get older, they often pressure parents to let them have a computer in their own room. Personally, I'd try to resist this. If you do give in, recognize the implications of that decision. It means that you will (a) have to talk to them more about what they do online (not something teenagers will relish) and (b) have to trust them more.

 Don't look in the obvious places A smart child will know that, if you occasionally look around the computer, they shouldn't leave things they don't want you to see in a file called 'myporn.doc'. Indeed, some sites and magazines advise kids to hide things they don't want their parents to see in files with forbiddingly technical names. If you want to keep an eye on things, the best bet is to look at the list of recently accessed documents.

2. Set some basic guidelines about net use in your home.

Think about how much time your kids spend online, where they access the net, and what kind of material they're allowed to access. Talk to your kids about this and, if your kids are a bit older, involve them in the process of setting guidelines.

- Set a basic daily limit on the amount of time your child spends online. You may want to allow them more time if they need to use it for homework. You may also want to limit use of the net until they've done their homework.

- If your child uses the net at friends' homes, talk to their parents about the kind of rules they've established about net use. It's no use you putting the computer in a family room and agreeing certain rules if your kids can go somewhere else and do what they like.

- Talk to your child about what kind of websites they are allowed to look at. You may want to limit them to sites listed in a kids' directory like Yahooligans or Kids Click. You may also want to talk to your child about the kinds of inappropriate material they might find online. With older children, it might be quite productive to talk about why you think certain material should be off-limits.

- If your child wants to chat, talk to them about which chatrooms they can use and what they can do there. Limit them to spaces that are moderated by an adult and not by an automated program. Check out the chatrooms your child wants to use and look at the kind of discussions that take place there.

Chat advice for parents There's lot of useful advice on the web about keeping kids safe in chatrooms. Try Smart Parent **http://www.smartparent.org.uk**, where you can find useful information and take part in a general campaign aimed at protecting kids who chat. Alternatively, have a look at Chat Danger **http://www.chatdanger.com**.

3. Set a few basic rules that your child must never break.

Here are some basic rules about the net to tell your children never to break:

Five rules for kids

1 Never give out personal/private information without your parents' permission.

2 Never give out your account password to someone who contacts you while you're online claiming to be from your ISP. It doesn't matter how official they sound. A genuine employee from your ISP/online service will never ask for information online.

3 Never meet an online friend in the real world unless your mum or dad or another adult you can trust is present.

4 Never reply to threatening/nasty emails or chat messages. Instead, save them, then show them to your mum or dad or another adult who can report them to the relevant authorities.

5 Tell someone if you encounter anyone or anything online that upsets or scares you.

Make sure your kids know that these rules are there for their safety. Make sure they understand why they should observe them. Obviously, there's a lot more to say about these rules – you'll find more details later in this section.

Internet family pledges A good way to make sure children take these guidelines and rules to heart is to formalize them in a kind of family pledge or agreement. Get your child to help you write it, then sign it along with them. It feels very American, I admit, but it will probably help. You'll find examples of the kind of thing you could do at Yahooligans **http://www.yahooligans.com/parents/createfamilypledge.html**.

4. Try to find time to surf with your child.

You may have to overcome significant obstacles to do this (grumpy teenagers determined to avoid your company, your own lack of time and so on). But persevere. By surfing with your child, you avoid making the net something he or she does in isolation. Talk to them about what they like to do on the net, let them show you things online and ask for their advice.

5. Teach your child net literacy and netiquette.

When it comes to knowing how to work certain programs, your child may not need any assistance. In fact, you might be able to pick up a few tips from them. But you will be able to help them learn a more general net literacy. This involves more than knowing how to navigate a particular site or how to use a search engine, and can help them avoid certain problems.

- Teach your child to be sceptical when they're on the web. It doesn't cost that much to make a website look good/official. Remind them to think about who put the site up and why they're telling you what they're telling you. Tell them to treat 'free gifts', 'huge cash prizes' and 'guaranteed money-making offers' with suspicion.

- Your child also needs to learn how to assess the people they encounter online. People aren't always who they claim to be online. They make out that they're better looking and cooler than they really are. Many men pretend to be women. Often this is pretty harmless. But your child needs to know that it goes on. They need to understand that they don't really know the people they meet via the net, that all they know is what they've been told.

- Make sure your child observes basic netiquette when they're in shared spaces online (e.g. discussion groups and chatrooms). There's plenty of specific advice about this on pages 128 and 150. Make sure they realize that these rules about conduct are there for a reason – to make the online world run smoothly and avoid fights and flare-ups.

- When it comes to netiquette, the most important lesson your child can learn is that there are people just like them behind those words that appear on the screen, that the things said online are read by real people and that things that could hurt people's feelings in the real world will prove similarly hurtful and upsetting online. 'Do as you would be done by' is something parents teach their kids in the real world. It's just as important online.

- Teach your child to stop and think before they press *SEND*. The net makes it easy to respond quickly to perceived insults and slights. This often makes things worse, creating full-blown online feuds out of things that weren't really disagreements in the first place.

Safety advice on the web You'll find lots of useful safety advice on the web. The Parents Information Network has a good guide at **http://www.pin.org.uk/safety/safetyset.htm**. Alternatively, have a look at the Government's net safety advice site at **http://safety.ngfl.gov.uk**.

Internet filtering software

When it comes to protecting their kids online, some parents will prefer to concentrate on setting rules and guidelines and talking to their children about the kinds of problems they may encounter online and how to cope with them. Others will want to back up these measures with technology, specifically internet filtering software. Net filters are now multi-purpose programs that you can customize and adapt to get the right level of protection for your child. They don't just block access to inappropriate sites and content. They also filter incoming and outgoing messages. Some only allow children to receive and send email to pre-approved addresses. They will block attachments and areas of the net that you deem to be off-limits (e.g. IRC or Usenet newsgroups). They will also monitor everything your child does online. And they can be used to let them access the net only at certain times of the day and for a certain period of time. So you can see how they could be very useful.

However, in the past net filtering software has come in for a lot of criticism. People have complained that:

- Net filters don't work that well. They often block sites that are fine and allow access to sites that are inappropriate.

- Net filters come with an inbuilt political bias. Often they follow a right-wing agenda and block sites relating to feminism and gay rights.

- Net filters encourage complacency in parents, who should be taking more of an interest in what their children do online and teaching them how to cope with inappropriate material/people.

- Net filters block safety information – e.g. about parental violence or incest – that should be available to children without their parents' knowledge.

All these criticisms are worth thinking about. However, the often-repeated suggestion that net filters are pointless because kids can find their way round them is no longer true. It might have been possible when these programs first appeared. But now these programs are much harder to crack. Serious hackers might be able to do it; most kids won't. Some critics take a more idealistic line on net filters. They argue that children have a right to be able to access all information and that filters are taking us closer to a world of tighter government control of free speech. They have a point where the use of net filters in public libraries is concerned. But where families are involved, it's down to parents to decide what kind of information their children can access. It's not something that should involve free speech campaigners.

Filterware critics One of the most determined filterware critics is Bennett Haselton. His Peacefire site **http://www.peacefire.org** has extensive reviews of different filterware programs, plus the latest news.

So how do net filters work?

- Some block sites deemed to be inappropriate. Others only allow access to pre-approved sites. They do this by referring to pre-prepared lists of approved and inappropriate sites.

- It's hard to keep these lists up-to-date so most programs also do real-time filtering. In other words, they review sites as children try to access them, looking for particular words or phrases.

- If a child tries to look at a site that is off-limits, the net filter tells them they can't access it, via an Alert screen. Some software is set up to work without your child being aware. These programs just flash up a general error message.

The best known net filtering programs are Cyberpatrol **http://www.cyberpatrol.com**, Cybersitter **http://www.cybersitter.com** and NetNanny **http://www.netnanny.com**. Check their websites for detailed information about how each works. Download the free demos from the site and try them out. It's fair to say that they're all a lot better than they used to be, but none of them will offer complete protection. You can't just set up a net filter then sit back and relax while your kids get online. You still need to take an interest and keep a look-out.

If you're trying to choose the right filter for you and your family, here are a few things you should think about:

- If a program works by using a list of inappropriate/bad sites, are you allowed to see it and modify it? Can you remove sites you think are fine and add others you don't like?

- How do the people behind the net filter decide what constitutes a bad site? Who does the monitoring and are they trained properly?

- How much does it cost to update the list and how often do you need to do it?

- If a program works via an approved/good list of sites, the same concerns apply. How often is it updated? How are sites selected? Can you add sites you like and take off others you don't?

- How does the program's real time filtering work? Does it look for naughty words in context rather than just apparently naughty words? The latter can lead to problems.

- Say you have two kids – a fifteen year-old and a nine year-old. You'll want different levels of protection for each. You won't want to buy different programs for each. Can a program be set up to offer different levels of protection for different users?

- Will the program in question filter/block real-time online chat? Can it be set up to block outgoing messages containing information you specify – for example, your telephone number and address?

Stealth filtering and monitoring Some filter programs can be set up so that children don't know their access is being blocked. Personally, I think it's better to tell kids that their access is being blocked and explain why you're doing it. Similarly, using net filters to monitor everything your child does online, from the sites they visit to the things they say in chatrooms, can cause problems. Older children really resent being monitored in detail.

There are some other net filtering programs that are aimed more at providing a general service for kids. Surf Monkey **http://www.surfmonkey.com** and Zeeks **http://www.zeeks.com** offer net filters, companion web sites and a range of other services. Once you download and install Surf Monkey's browsing software, your kids will be able to interact with Surf Monkey himself, an on-screen cartoon character that guides kids round the net and reads their email to them. Both services are worth investigating. However, you may not need to buy new software to filter your child's net access. AOL and some family ISPs offer their own filtering programs. AOL's parental controls, in particular, are quite useful. Look for the toolbar button on their opening screen and then follow the directions for setting them up.

> **Filterware reviews** You'll find an excellent guide to filtering software and some detailed product reviews at the Parents Information Network site **http://www.pin.org.uk**.

Internet Explorer allows for some web filtering. If you want to try it out:

1 Select the *TOOLS* menu, then *INTERNET OPTIONS*, then click the *CONTENT* tab.

2 Click the *ENABLE* button in the *CONTENT ADVISOR* section. You'll go to a *CONTENT ADVISOR* dialog box.

3 Once you set a password, you can use a little slider control to set acceptable levels as far as Language, Nudity, Sex and Violence are concerned. You can also set up a list of approved sites and create passwords that allow access to restricted material.

In the Mac version of Internet Explorer:

1 Select *EDIT*, then *PREFERENCES*, then in the *WEB BROWSER* section, click on *RATINGS*

Don't expect too much from this though. Browser filters only really work with sites that have assessed themselves using either the RSACi ratings or the Safe Surf ratings. Most adult sites haven't bothered to get a rating. So your browser won't know to block them. For more information on these ratings sytems, go to the Internet Content Rating Association **http://www.icra.org** or try the Safe Surf page **http://www.safesurf.com**.

Both pages have more information on how to set up content filters in the two big browsers.

Incidentally, your browser will let you keep an eye on what your child has been looking at on the web. It records where they've been (in History), stores pages they've visited in the cache, retains addresses entered in its location bar and has a file filled with cookies – special identifying files placed by some sites on your hard disk (more about these later). If you want to look at the cookies on a browser:

- **In Internet Explorer:**
  1 Your cookies will be in a *COOKIES* folder in the general *WINDOWS* directory.

- **In Netscape 6:**
  1 Select the *TASKS* menu, then *PRIVACY AND SECURITY*.
  2 Then choose *COOKIE MANAGER*, then the *VIEW STORED COOKIES* option.

Smart kids will know about all this. Be suspicious if you find a completely clear History and an empty cache after a couple of hours' surfing.

Dealing with specific problems

As mentioned earlier in this section, there are several key risks your kids may face online. Tackling them usually involves talking to your kids, setting rules and guidelines and using filtering software. But each problem presents particular challenges you need to know about.

Inappropriate information

In general, you probably have to accept that your kids will have a look at inappropriate material online. Personally, I think it only really becomes a problem if they do it persistently and become obsessed with a particular kind of site. However, what your kids see online should be your decision. Remember, you're still the parent online. Internet filters can help here but you need to back them up by talking to your child and keeping a discreet eye on what they do.

• **Pornography.** Most kids will be tempted to have a look at adult sites. Many will quickly get bored by what they find. And at many sites they won't be able to get past the front pages. Most responsible porn sites run adult verification checks and require credit card details from potential users. That said, even these sites showcase free samples of what's on offer inside. And there are sites offering pornographic material for free. Internet filters do a reasonable job of blocking access to porn sites, but they're not perfect. So accept that your child might be curious about this and talk to your child about adult material online and why you think it's not suitable for them.

- **Hate speech/intolerance**. Unfortunately, there are lots of sites online that spout racist bilge and bigoted nonsense. Again, children may be curious to have a look at these. Many are blocked by some of the net filters. Again, you should talk talk to your child about these sites and their views. Explain why prejudice and discrimination are wrong. Explain the damage they do.

- **Gore.** There are sites online that specialize in showcasing 'gross' pictures. This can cover everything from pictures of strange medical conditions to autopsy/accident photos. Some children seem much more drawn to this stuff than pornography. Again, you have to accept that your child (especially as they get older) will be curious about this kind of thing. Internet filters will block access to many of these sites. But once again, talk to your child about this material. Explain that the real-life pictures these sites show involved real-life pain – they're not like horror films.

- **Disinformation/Conspiracy theories/Hoaxes** Though there's plenty of useful and reliable information on the net, there's also tons of rubbish. And there's lots of information that is tricked up to look official and reliable, but isn't. The best protection against this is to teach your child net literacy as suggested before

- **Dangerous information** There are sites online that feature directions on making bombs. The real problem with these sites, according to those who know, is that the recipes they feature are inaccurate and thus even more dangerous than they might be. Here, net filtering software should help. But if you think your child might be drawn to this, you should talk to them about it and explain the dangers

Obviously, use your discretion when it comes to talking to children about the kinds of inappropriate material they might find online. You don't want to scare or upset younger children, or alert them to things they didn't know about. That said, as children get older, it will help to be honest with them about what's online, to discuss why you don't want them to access certain material. Treating them as adults may make them less likely to waste too much time on so-called adult material. Finally, children who are feeling vulnerable in real life, kids who are unhappy at home or school, who can't make friends or get on, often find themselves drawn to inappropriate material online.

Clearing your machine If you check out online porn using the same software as your kids, it's your business. However, your browser can make it their business. The URLs will be in History and there will be cookies in your browser identifying whoever is using the browser as a porn consumer. Some sites may then target X-rated advertising at that browser. So, if you want to protect your kids, clear History and get rid of any offending cookies.

Protecting your child's privacy

The net may allow a superficial kind of anonymity – one that lets people mess around in chatrooms pretending to be someone else. But at a more fundamental level, much of what you do online is accessible to all sorts of people who know how to look. As privacy activists have pointed out, the net is redefining the nature of privacy, allowing governments and corporations greater access to ordinary people's lives. These days, much of what you do on the net can be tracked and analysed. All this is problematic enough for adults who use the net. Many parents find it especially worrying that their children's privacy might be at risk while they use the net.

Online privacy For information on protecting your own privacy online, try the Electronic Privacy Information Centre at **http://epic.org**. For a British perspective, try Cyber Rights and Cyber Liberties site **http://www.cyber-rights.org**.

Where your child's privacy is concerned, you need to focus your concern on two areas:

- Your child might give away personal/private information that lets cyberpredators target them online and in real life.

- Your child might give away information that marketers can use for commercial gain. It can be used to create targeted ads that children will find very hard to resist.

So how should you protect your child's personal information?

- Make sure your child understands what information they should keep private. In general, it's anything that could be used to target them online and off, which means their real name, your address and telephone number, their ISP account password, their email address and their school address.

- Teach them about the different ways they can give away personal information. They can do it via email signatures, personal profiles posted to websites, via their homepages, via contributions they make to mailing lists and discussion groups.

- Screen names can also reveal their gender, so encourage them to pick something abstract and non-specific.

- It's easy to give away important information via an innocent conversation in a chatroom. Chatting with someone about a school team and where it played recently can, when cross-referenced with other sources, yield up information that determined cyberpredators can use. Try to teach your child how easy it is to give things away without realizing.

- If you set them up properly, some internet filters can stop kids from sending important information – telephone numbers, addresses and so on – in emails, newsgroup postings and chat.

- Make sure that they don't hand over any personal information to websites without asking you first. Many kids' sites require kids to register before they can use them properly. Before you let your child hand over any data, check the site's privacy policy. Find out why they need certain information and whether they're going to sell it on to junk mailers and the like. If you're unhappy in any way, don't sign up with the site.

- Many sites offer free gifts to kids who hand over information about their likes and dislikes. Teach your child that you never really get something for nothing. Make sure that, however tempting the loot on offer, they come to you first before handing over any information.

- Teach your child to take care with mailing lists and discussion groups. Many of these are publicly accessible. Many of these groups archive the messages posted to them. These can be searched by people who want to find out about what your child has said. Some spammers harvest addresses from these groups too – more on this shortly.

The web can pose particular problems where privacy is concerned. Many sites surreptitiously gather information about the people who use them. They do this via cookies, little identifying text files that some sites place on your computer when you visit them. When you go back to a particular site, it looks at the cookie to find out what you did there before. It also adds more information. Many sites use cookies to log your personal preferences. Shopping sites use cookies so that they can remember what you bought before and direct you to other things you might like. While this sounds fine, you might feel less comfortable about companies snooping around your child's cookies, building a database on them and then sharing it with others who use the information to target advertising at your child.

Most sites talk about if and why they use cookies in their privacy policies. If you're unhappy with their explanation about why they use them, if it seems to you that they might be collecting too much information, you can get your browser to refuse cookies.

- **In Internet Explorer:**

  1 Select the *TOOLS* menu then *INTERNET OPTIONS* and then the *SECURITY* tab.

  2 Underneath 'Click on a web content zone…', select *INTERNET* then press the *CUSTOM LEVEL* button.

  3 In the *SECURITY SETTINGS* dialog box, scroll down to the section on *COOKIES* and select the relevant option.

- **In Netscape 6:**

  1 Select the *EDIT* menu, then *PREFERENCES*

  2 You'll find the *COOKIES* section in the *PRIVACY AND SECURITY HIERARCHY*.

  3 In the *COOKIES* section you can choose whether to enable or block all cookies.

- **In the Mac version of Internet Explorer:**

  1 Select the *EDIT* menu, then *PREFERENCES*.

  2 Then in the *RECEIVING FILES* section, click on *COOKIES* then select *NEVER ACCEPT* via the drop-down menu.

Cookies aren't the only threat to privacy on the web. As you surf, your browser reveals all sorts of other bits of information about you. To find out what exactly, visit Privacy.net at **http://privacy.net/anonymizer/**. Some sites use a programming language called JavaScript to copy your email address while you're browsing. You can stop this by not entering your email address into the relevant sections of your browser. That means you won't be able to use it for email. Alternatively, change the settings on your browser to block JavaScript.

- In Internet Explorer:
  1 Select the *TOOLS* menu, then *INTERNET OPTIONS* and then the *SECURITY* tab.
  2 Underneath 'Click on a web content zone…', select *INTERNET*, then press the *CUSTOM LEVEL* button.
  3 In the *SECURITY SETTINGS* dialog box, scroll down to the *JAVA* section and choose to disable it.

- In Netscape 6:
  1 Select the *EDIT* menu, then *PREFERENCES*, then *ADVANCED* and look for the *JAVA* section.

- In the Mac version of Internet Explorer:
  1 Select the *EDIT* menu, then *PREFERENCES*.
  2 In the *WEB BROWSER* section, click on *JAVA*, then make the changes you want in the *JAVA OPTIONS* box.

Find out about cookies
Cookie Central **http://www.cookiecentral.com** has more information on cookies, plus links to programs you can use to control them, for example Cookie Cutter, Cookie Crusher and Cookie Pal. You can also find some links to these on EPIC's privacy tools page **http://www.epic.org/privacy/tools.html**. Many let you specify which cookies you want to accept, so with your help, your child can benefit from personalization at some sites and avoid problems at others.

Cyberpredators

Perhaps the most obvious downside of the open access offered by the net is that it makes it much easier for paedophiles to make contact with children. Before the net, it was harder. Paedophiles had to find jobs looking after or working with children. The net has changed that. It makes it relatively easy for determined paedophiles to communicate with children via the screen of a PC. However, their ultimate aim is still to get access to a child in the real world, and that remains difficult, especially if parents and guardians remain vigilant. So how do 'cyberpredators' operate online? In general they start by trying to build a friendship with a child. Often they look for children who seem vulnerable and unhappy. Often they pretend to be a child of the same age but the opposite sex. As the relationship deepens, they may get hold of a child's telephone number and call or send gifts. Gradually, they will start sexual conversations. Some will send children examples of child porn, with the aim of suggesting that sexual behaviour for kids is normal and that 'everyone's doing it'. Often they send their targets Polaroid cameras and then suggest they take suggestive pictures of themselves. Their ultimate aim is always to move to a real-world meeting with the child.

So what should you do to protect your child?

- Make sure they have taken to heart the lessons about giving away important personal information contained in the previous section.

- Use net filters to stop them from sending personal details via email and chat messages.

- Make sure they realize that people they know online aren't the same as real-world friends. They don't really 'know' them. In a way, online friends always remain strangers.

- Talk about the problem with them – though try to do it without alarming them. Tell them what to look out for. Explain the way that cyberpredators work, as detailed above.

- Keep an eye on your child. Are they spending an awful lot of time online? Have they developed a strong online friendship that seems to take precedence over real-world relationships? If they have, ask to see some of the mail involved. You may be able to spot something dubious that they haven't noticed. Check your telephone bills to see if they're regularly calling certain numbers.

- If they have developed a friendship with someone online, make sure they know they should never meet this person unless you or a responsible adult is present.

- If their online friend complains and refuses to meet them unless they're on their own, be very suspicious. Make sure they know that this is suspicious behaviour, not natural teenage dislike of parents/grown-ups getting in the way.

- If you do agree to a meeting, make sure it's in a public place. If things go wrong – if your child is stood up, don't go straight home. You may be followed. Instead go to another public place. Don't let your kids go off on their own after a failed meeting.

Cyberstalking

The 'cyberstalkers' who harass children online often turn out to be other children. Many fire off nasty emails and the like to see what kind of reaction they can get. They play out fantasies online and often don't really understand the hurt they're causing. Most don't do it out of any real maliciousness or out of any real animus against their targets. That said, some cyberstalking has its roots in failed online relationships, in net friendships that have turned sour. Problems often start in chatrooms or on discussion groups. So what should your child do to avoid problems?

- Guard their personal information carefully. Don't put contact information on webpages or in sig files. Don't circulate personal information in messages sent to discussion groups. If your child posts a personal profile to a particular site, make sure they don't include important information or contact details.

- In chatrooms, your child's chat software should be configured so that it doesn't reveal anything important or real about them. Make sure they use a non-gender-specific nickname.

- Teach them to avoid flirting and suggestive talk in chatrooms. This can lead to the wrong sort of attention and can cause problems that lead to cyberstalking.

- Teach your child to use the *IGNORE* function on their chat software to make irritating/threatening people in a chatroom disappear.

- If problems persist, your child should report them to the people running the chatroom and to you. They shouldn't respond in kind. This usually only makes things worse.

- If someone sends your child persistent abusive mail, try to set up mail filters to block it. Make sure your child doesn't respond in kind. Many cyberstalkers take this as a sign that they're having an effect and they carry on. Instead, they should save the mail and show it you. You should send it to their tormentor's ISP to complain (try mailing **postmaster@ispname.com**).

- If their mail gives a false name and address, look at the header for more information about them and their messages. Get help from your ISP.

- Ultimately, if you're worried, especially if things look like they might spill over into the real world – e.g. if your child starts getting threatening telephone calls, get the police involved.

- Remember – your child is perfectly capable of cyberstalking another child. If they do, you may only find out about it when their parents get in touch with you to complain. So anticipate any potential problems in advance. Make sure your kids realize how upsetting this is and how easy it often is to track down the people doing it.

Spam

Most net users hate spam, or unwanted junk email. It's pretty obvious why. Spam costs time and money. Deleting it can be a lengthy process. And in contrast to real world junk mail, the recipient actually pays for the privilege of getting spam. Spam is particularly troubling for parents. It puts inappropriate material in their kids' mailboxes – everything from ads for porn sites (with pictures and links) and fraudulent get-rich-quick offers to fake charity appeals and other cons designed to trick the gullible into handing over money. Not the kind of thing you want your kids to see when they log on. Worse, spam can make parents them trust their kids less. Many, finding spam for porn sites in their children's mailboxes, assume that they must have done something to get that kind of mail. They haven't. Everyone gets this kind of stuff. It isn't proof that they've been looking for porn on the net. The important thing with spam is not to let it take over your life. You can do certain things to minimize the problems it causes. But you can't make it go away completely. So do what you can and then get on with your online life.

• Teach your child not to read it. If they do read it, they shouldn't believe anything in it. It's all rubbish.

• Spammers assemble their mailing lists with addresses harvested from discussion groups and webpages. To counter this, set up two mail accounts for your child. Keep one private and make one the publicly available address, the one they can put on their webpages and use for discussion groups. That way, all the spam should at least be channelled into one account.

- There are all sorts of specialist spam blocker programs you could try. Though these are a nice idea, they never really work that well and can take up a lot of time and money. Instead, use your standard mail program to set up filters that will block spam or divert it to the trash folder. They won't block everything, but they're better than nothing.

- Internet filters can help too. Some spam includes links to porn sites. Some filters will block those links, so if your child clicks those links they won't be able to access the site in question.

- At the end of spam, you'll usually see a return address you're invited to use if you want to stop receiving mail. Don't reply. If you do, you'll get even more spam. Spammers often do this to find out if a particular account is still live.

- Most spammers don't supply a working email address. In that case, complain to their ISP (for example, send email to **postmaster@ispname.com**). If all the addresses on the spam are faked, you can find the real address from the mail header – Junkbusters **http://www.junkbusters.com** has some tips on this.

Anti-spam resources You can find out lots more about dealing with spam online. For legal angles and links, try the Coalition Against Unsolicited Commercial Email **http://www.euro.cauce.org**. Alternatively, try Fight Spam on the Internet **http://spam.abuse.net/** for links to some useful tools.

....
Viruses
....

Viruses spread via email have received a lot of attention over the last few years. You need to make sure your child is aware of the problems these can cause and how they work. Typically, a mail-borne virus like Melissa is spread via attachments. An email arrives in your mailbox, with an attached file. If you then delete that file, you'll be fine. This sort of virus isn't activated unless you open a particular attachment. If you do, the classic mail-borne virus will then send itself to everyone on your address book. Teach your child about this. But don't forget that lots of viruses are still spread by sharing floppy discs. Make sure they know about this.

So what can you do to protect your computer from infection?

- Get a good anti-virus program and update it regularly. Teach your child how to use it. Make sure you and they always virus-check programs before installing them. There are three big anti-virus programs: Doctor Solomon's AntiVirus **http://www.drsolomon.com/**, Norton AntiVirus **http://www.symantec.com**, and McAfee's Virus-Scan **http://www.nai.com**.

- Teach your child to be wary of email attachments. If they arrive from someone you don't know, dump them in the bin. If they arrive from people you do know, there still may be a problem. So if a message turns up unexpectedly, with slightly stilted subject lines or messages, contact the friend who sent it to find out if it's genuine before you open the attachment.

- Microsoft critics say that you can minimise the risk of infection from viruses like the Lovebug by not using Outlook Express. So far, these viruses have tended to be targeted at Microsoft programs. It might help, but it's no guarantee. If you do use Microsoft software, make sure that you visit their site regularly and download the various security patches they issue to deal with different viruses.

- Teach your child about the problems caused by the fake virus alert – mail warning of an email virus that will infect your computer if you download and read it. These messages are viruses of a sort: psychological viruses that cause you to waste valuable time wondering whether they're true. Your child should ignore them and not pass them on.

> **Virus myths** For a very useful guide to online hoaxes, try the About.com Urban Legends page **http://urbanlegends.about.com** and look for the Net Hoaxes and Virus Hoaxes links. For news about real viruses (and lots of stuff about information war in general), try The Crypt **http://sun.soci.niu.edu/~crypt/**.

Online pranks

The net offers teenagers all sorts of new ways to get up to mischief. Much of what they get up to is an online extension of the kind of teasing that takes place in the real world. But things can quickly get serious online. If they do, you may be the one who ends up footing the bill (literally in some cases). So what might your child get up to?

- If they gain access to your credit card details, they can use them to buy themselves books, videos and CDs online.

- They might gain access to someone's account and then post out-of-character/provocative messages. The kids who do this sometimes send fake emails to their target's friends, with the aim of winding them up. Sometimes, they post messages to public chatrooms and discussion groups. Sometimes, they use the access to post fake personal profiles on ISP websites.

Wind-ups like this can result in an awful lot of unwanted attention, e.g. a fake message that says that the sender is interested in sex. If these fake messages include information that identifies where the supposed sender lives, things become much more serious. So what should you do to prevent things getting out of hand?

- Make sure your child doesn't share their net account details/passwords with their friends.

- Keep your net account details/password hidden. Change your password regularly.

- Keep your financial details (in particular your credit card information) away from prying eyes. Check your credit card statements carefully.

- Teach your child that pranks can do real harm to those on the receiving end. Make sure that they realize that online pranks involving suggestive sexual detail can lead to dangerous situations.

- Keep an eye on what your child's friends get up to when they're using the net in your home, via your account. Similarly your child might use the net account at a friend's home to get up to mischief. Talk to friends' parents about the possibility of this kind of thing happening.

Hackers

Some people seem convinced that once you get online, hordes of malicious hackers will seek you out and make your life a misery. The truth is that most hackers spend their time either trying to make other hackers' lives a misery or trying to break into government/military computers, both in an attempt to prove how hardcore they are. Generally, they won't bug you if you don't bug them. That said, you should take certain precautions:

- Teach your child to take care in certain online locations, especially IRC chatrooms. If they're in a chatroom and someone tells them to type a particular command, they should never do it. It may let them take over your computer.

- Your child should be careful with software downloaded from sites that seem less than reputable. There have been reports in the past of programs designed to let hackers charge telephone bills to users who installed them.

- Broadband connections to the net are 'always on' and so are visible on the network to anyone poking around in the right places. As a result, they are theoretically more vulnerable to intruders than the standard dial-up connections. So you should probably take certain security precautions. Go back to page 191 for some specific tips.

There's a chance your child might take up hacking. How can you tell? To be honest, there isn't any obvious checklist of telltale signs. But there are a few things you should look out for:

- It's hard to hack in the lounge, with parents who are keeping an eye on what's going on. So if your child has the computer in their own room and uses it for long periods of time, you might want to check what they're up to.

- Certain areas of the net are more popular with hackers – in particular IRC chatrooms. Hackers also use FTP programs and sites more than the average net user. If your computer shows signs that they've been using IRC and FTP, you might want to talk to them about it.

An interest in hacking isn't necessarily a bad thing. The media tends to portray hackers as irresponsible info-vandals. However, the word 'hacker' was first used to refer to a skilled programmer who liked to mess around with early computers. These old-school hackers helped build the net and dismiss the more destructive hackers as 'crackers'. So if your child seems to be drifting in that direction, perhaps the best thing to do is to try to channel their energies.

- Talk to them about hacking and why some forms of it are wrong. Point out that accessing government/corporate computers and circulating viruses can have serious consequences.

- Try to point them towards more traditional hacking. For example, the Open Source movement mentioned on page 84 is a good place for computer-mad teens to develop their programming skills and think about computers and their place in the world.

Copyright on the net

Digital technology makes it easy to make copies of things. The net makes it easy to share those copies with other people. As a result, some theorists argue that old intellectual property laws don't work any more online, and that we need to work out a new way of compensating people for the content they create. Against this, there have been signs that, under the cover of responding to the net and digital technology, various corporations are trying to extend intellectual property laws in a way that would drastically curtail free public discussion. Certainly, over the last few years, both individual artists and creative industries as a whole have tried to take action against websites they claim are illegally using copyrighted material. It's understandable when musicians get angry at people trading their music online without paying them anything. Big media companies trying to close down film fan sites created by children because they infringe their intellectual property is another thing. But it does happen. In the run-up to the release of the *Harry Potter* film, fan sites, some created by kids, came under pressure from the film's makers. In general, these disputes are resolved amicably enough. That said, no one likes to get letters from lawyers. So what can you do to avoid potential problems?

- Teach your child to think about the copyright status of material you use online and why it's important. Talk to them about who created certain images and songs and why it's important that they be recompensed for their efforts.

- More specifically, if your child uses pictures scanned from magazines on their homepage, it's likely that, legally, they belong to someone else. So get permission or give credits and indicate who owns the copyright.

- If your child re-posts material to a discussion group or webpage – an interesting newspaper story, say – make sure they give the appropriate credits.

- If possible, your child should check with the authors before they send one discussion group posting on to a new discussion group. It will probably be fine, but since they will own the copyright, you should check anyway.

- There's lots of pirated material circulating online – software, games, music and even video. Make sure your child knows that downloading this stuff has serious implications – ask them how they would feel if someone helped themselves to their creative work.

 Plagiarism sites Warn your child about using sites that supply pre-written essays and dissertations. These sites are often American and are more popular over there. But you should be aware of them. Teachers are now wise to them and find it relatively easy to spot an essay from one of the plagiarism sites. So make sure your child knows that this is cheating, that they will probably be found out and that it could have serious consequences.

Libel online

Over the last few years, people have been successful in suing for libel over things that were said online, though, if the truth be told, things are still a little unclear. But in general, you should make your kids aware of the potential problems posed by libel and slander. Obviously, this isn't something that's going to concern younger children. Their name-calling isn't likely to lead to disputes that end up in court (though given the excesses of the legal profession in America, you never know). The real potential problem here is teenagers. The net gives them a great platform to say what they think and there is a chance they may go too far. If you want to avoid hassle:

• Teach your child to think before they sound off on the web, in discussion groups, mailing lists and chatrooms.

• Make sure your child understands that people do take offence, and that if they feel hurt enough by things that are said on screen, they may take legal action.

- In America, problems have been caused by children putting up websites attacking particular teachers. This can lead to expulsion. I don't think this has happened yet in the UK, but look out for it. Make sure your child doesn't take classroom grievances into a public arena without consulting you first and giving you the chance to sort things out.

6

Essential clicks
for parents

The net isn't just for kids. It's for you too. You'll find lots of useful advice about parenting online. You can swap ideas and get support from other parents. You can research medical problems, buy birthday presents and book family holidays online – if you know where to look. That's where the following directory comes in. Of course, the best thing with the net is to log on and search for the things you want. You may be surprised by just how many sites there are that aim to help parents. But it's also useful to have an idea of what's out there, so you can focus your surfing a little. Hence the Essential Clicks for Parents. As with the Essential Clicks for Kids, the idea is to highlight some of the better sites, draw your attention to pages you might not find otherwise and give you a few hints about where to search further. Again, where appropriate, I've added some general tips about searching for sites covering a particular area. Incidentally, if you want to catch up with the Guardian's latest coverage of parental issues, it appears every Wednesday in the G2 supplement. You can read it online too – go to **http://www.guardian.co.uk** and click on the G2 link.

Parenting portals

If you visited some of the kids' portal sites mentioned in Section 3 (page 208) with your children, you may have noticed that many have special parents' areas, which feature news and advice, often about net safety. Many of these sections are useful enough, but you'll probably get more out of the growing number of portals aimed specifically at parents. Some of these are magazine-based – they specialize mainly in news and features. Others offer 'community' elements too – discussion groups and chatrooms where parents can share ideas with each other. Some also have useful interactive tools – birth calendars and the like.

BBC Parenting http://www.bbc.co.uk/health/parenting. This BBC site has information on coping with babies and toddlers, illnesses, immunisation, and lots of useful contact links.

E-Parents http://www.e-parents.org. A magazine site put up by the National Family and Parenting Institute, this has news, celebrity parent interviews, advice on net safety, families and the law and more.

Flametree http://www.flametree.co.uk. This site aims to promote a better work/life balance for people and business. There's some good parenting tips in the Home and Family section.

Home Dad http://www.homedad.org.uk. An online magazine for dads who stay at home to bring up their kids. Aside from features and information, this has discussion groups and regular chat sessions.

Iparenting.com http://www.iparenting.com. A big American parenting portal, but still worth a look. This has community elements (e.g. discussion groups), information and useful tools – pregnancy calendars and the like.

MumsNet http://www.mumsnet.com. An excellent parent-generated site of product reviews, expert advice and general support. Not just for mums.

Parents Online **http://www.parents.org.uk**. A portal for British parents aimed at people with children of primary school age, this has useful advice on health, education and going out with kids.

Parent Talk **http://www.parenttalk.co.uk**. A magazine site, this supplements a good mix of features and jokey columns with discussion groups and shopping advice.

Parentline Plus **http://www.parentlineplus.org.uk**. The site of the UK-based charity that aims to offer support to 'anyone parenting a child'. This has lots of advice on negotiating tricky situations, from truancy to general teenage rebellion.

Practical Parenting **http://www.practicalparent.org.uk**. A useful site that sets out to offer practical advice to parents and professionals involved with kids.

UK Parents **http://www.ukparents.co.uk**. Another portal that serves up all sorts of parental advice, plus reviews, features, shopping, discussion boards and a nice clear design. Very useful.

Lone parents

Planet One Parent http://www.planetoneparent.com. Aims to be a comprehensive directory of useful information for single parents, which means everything from child-raising tips to advice on going on dates again.

Gingerbread http://www.gingerbread.org.uk. The online presence of the well-known support organization for lone parents, this has lots of useful information, contact numbers, addresses and more.

Net advice and safety

Childnet International **http://www.childnet-int.org/**. Childnet is an organization that aims to make the net a better place for kids. Its site has useful advice on safety and access, among other things.

Cyberangels **http://www.cyberangels.org**. You'll find loads of information about keeping your kids safe online at this site. Some of it has an American focus, but it's still useful, as is their companion site WiredKids **http://www.wiredkids.org**.

Internet Watch Foundation **http://www.iwf.org.uk**. The organization set up by British net industry types to tackle the problem of child porn online, this is the place to report illegal material you may find. It also has some useful safe surfing tips.

Net Mom **http://www.netmom.com**. The companion site to the American net guide, The Internet Kids and Family Yellow Pages, this has some useful advice and links for parents.

Parents Information Network **http://www.pin.org.uk**. An excellent site, this has loads of advice about computers and the net, from software reviews to safe surfing tips, analysis of net filtering software and advice on using the net to help with homework.

Smart Parent **http://www.smartparent.org.uk/**. A site focused on tackling the problems associated with kids and online chat – sign a petition here and get advice.

Babies and toddlers

B4Baby http://www.b4baby.com. A site aimed at those trying to become parents and people who have just become parents, this has an engaging mix of news, features and product reviews.

Babyworld http://www.babyworld.co.uk. A useful magazine site packed with information on pregnancy and babies and lots of product reviews and buying guides.

Baby Centre http://www.babycentre.co.uk. An excellent site covering pregnancy, birth and new babies, this has loads of useful tools to help you get ready for the big event and cope afterwards.

Baby City http://www.babycity.co.uk. Yet another magazine site, updated monthly, aimed at parents who are just getting started – this has the usual mix of reviews, news, tips on names and more.

Baby Directory http://www.babydirectory.com. An online directory of baby resources across the UK, this is linked to print publications of the same name.

Homebirth http://www.homebirth.org.uk. If you're thinking of having your baby at home, check in here for useful information and links.

Jane's Breastfeeding Resources http://www.breastfeeding.co.uk. Despite the web address, this isn't just focused on breastfeeding, but has general childbirth resources too.

National Childbirth Trust http://www.nctpregnancyandbabycare.com/. The NCT site has loads of general info, alongside information about events and meetings in your area. Very useful.

Small Folk http://www.smallfolk.co.uk. A useful general site about babies, apparently endorsed by the Great Ormond Street Children's Hospital, with the usual mix of information, shopping and community areas.

Tamba http://www.tamba.org.uk. The website of the Twins and Multiple Births Association – come here for advice about coping with twins, triplets and more.

Childcare

BestBear http://www.bestbear.co.uk/parents.htm. If you're looking for a nanny, au pair, or a baby-sitter, check in here and get local recommendations, plus lots of general advice. Very useful.

Child Care Link http://www.childcarelink.gov.uk. Get childcare information for your area from this directory site – which means advice on how to find childcarers, plus useful links and addresses.

Daycare Trust http://www.daycaretrust.org.uk. The website of the national childcare charity, this has lots of advice on choosing and paying for childcare.

International Au Pairs Association http://www.iapa.org. If you're thinking of getting an au pair, you can find out more and apply via this site.

DFES Nanny http://www.dfes.gov.uk/nanny/. Government advice on choosing a nanny, from the Department for Education and Skills.

National Childminding Association http://www.ncma.org.uk. Check in here for advice about looking for a registered childminder.

Sitters http://www.sitters.co.uk. The website of one of the big baby-sitting agencies – you can either book a baby-sitter here or do some research and then telephone them.

Education

There are loads of education-related sites online – the following selection is designed to give you a hint of what's out there. One area that might be interesting to look into is sites put up by schools. There are more and more of these, and they give you a good idea of the role the net is playing at school.

Books Unlimited http://books.guardian.co.uk/. The *Guardian's* books site has a useful section on kid's literature, which features advice on buying books for kids, recent reviews and links.

Bullying Online http://www.bullying.co.uk/. A great site for everyone suffering from bullying, this has advice for parents and kids, sample letters parents can use and much more.

DFES Parents http://www.dfes.gov.uk/parents/index.cfm. It used to be the Department for Education and Employment., but now it's the Department for Education and Skills. This is its site for parents – loads of information about choosing schools, helping with homework and more.

The Good Schools Guide http://www.goodschoolsguide.co.uk. The online companion to the best-selling print guide. Search for information on schools in your area. To get the full version, you'll need to subscribe – or buy the book.

Education Guardian http://education.guardian.co.uk. This *Guardian* site has news and views on all areas of the education system. Go to the Schools section and you'll find some very useful links to sites concerned with education/parenting and more.

Home Education UK http://www.home-education.org.uk/. Parents planning to educate their kids at home will find useful information and links here.

Independent Schools Information Service http://www.isis.org.uk. An online directory that lets you search for details on independent schools in your area.

Love Life http://www.lovelife.uk.com/. A sexual health/education site aimed at older teens – this may help out when it comes to talking to your kids about sex.

Office for Standards in Education http://www.ofsted.gov.uk. Come here to download and check out the inspection reports on schools in your area.

National Curriculum Online http://www.nc.uk.net. Although this government site is aimed at teachers, parents can use it to find out more about what your kids do all day at school.

Schoolsnet http://www.schoolsnet.com. A huge educational portal aimed at parents, teachers and kids – parents might find the school reviews and the revision tips useful.

Going Out

Ananova http://www.ananova.com/whatson/. A useful all-purpose listings site that should come in handy if you're planning family outings.

Family Travel http://www.family-travel.co.uk. A very useful resource for planning family holidays, this has travel advice, reviews and reports. To get the full site you will need to subscribe.

Farm Stay UK http://www.farm-holidays.co.uk. The online presence of a network of over a thousand UK farms offering family holidays. Very useful.

5 Minutes Away http://www.5minutesaway.co.uk/. If you have to drive a long way with the kids, research your journey at this site, which tells you about facilities 'five minutes away' from motorway junctions.

Kids Around Town http://www.kidsaroundtown.co.uk/. An online what's on guide for parents and kids, this covers places to go, party organization, after-school activities and more.

Planit4Kids http://www.planit4kids.com. Pick your area and this online directory will serve up a selection of news/reviews about events/places to go near you.

Recommended Cottages http://www.recommended-cottages.co.uk. If you're looking for a short break in the UK in a country cottage, you can research options at this site.

Ticketmaster UK http://www.ticketmaster.co.uk/. Research kids' events and shows here, then buy the tickets online.

What's On When http://www.whatsonwhen.com. A global listings site with surprisingly detailed coverage of the UK.

Wizziwiz http://www.wizziwiz.co.uk. An excellent, well-designed site featuring up-to-date listings info for kids, covering clubs, events, days out and more.

Health

Health sites have drawn some criticism from medical professionals and media types, worried about the quality of the information they serve up to anxious patients. It's true that you need to take care with some health-related sites. That said, the net can tell you an awful lot about certain conditions and diseases and, used sensibly, can help you get better care for you and your family. In particular, there are now lots of sites devoted to specific conditions and syndromes. A few are listed below. There wasn't the space to include more. But if you or your child is suffering from a particular condition, search online for material related to it. Apart from sites put up by official charities/foundations, you may also find sites run by parents of kids with the same condition, which are often great sources of information and support.

About.com Allergies http://allergies.about.com. A typically useful site from About.com, this points you to all sorts of (mostly American) resources connected to different allergies.

ADD/ADHD Online Support Group http://www.adders.org. Check in here to get information about AD/HD (Attention Deficit/Hyperactivity Disorder), contact other parents and find out about events/support groups.

Asthma http://www.asthma.org.uk. Download information about asthma, read the latest research and join the campaign to raise awareness about the condition.

Childline http://www.childline.org.uk. The Childline telephone line is obviously for children and young adults, but the website has some useful information for parents too.

Contact A Family http://www.cafamily.org.uk. The online home of a UK charity that aims to put parents of kids with special needs/disabilities in touch with other families in the same position.

National Deaf Children's Society http://www.ndcs.org.uk. You'll find information about childhood deafness here, along with details of NDCS's various family services.

Diabetes UK http://www.diabetes.org.uk. The website of the leading UK charity for people with diabetes. Find out more about the condition and how to manage it here.

The Dyslexia Institute http://www.dyslexia-inst.org.uk. A good place to come to find out more about dyslexia and how to teach children with the condition.

The Dyspraxia Foundation http://www.emmbrook.demon.co.uk/dysprax/homepage.htm. The online home of an organization set up to support families affected by so-called 'clumsy child syndrome'. Find out more about the condition here.

The Enuresis Resource Information Centre http://www.eric.org.uk. Enuresis is the medical term for bedwetting – you'll find information for parents and kids coping with this problem here.

Foundation for the Study of Infant Deaths http://www.sids.org.uk/fsid. Find out about the latest research into cot deaths and get advice, help and support here.

Health Links http://www.healthlinks.net. A huge American health portal, this has a directory of useful links, community areas, health-related classified ads and more.

Immunization http://www.immunisation.org.uk. Health Promotion England's immunization site has information and research on the various childhood injections, including the much talked about MMR jab. Incidentally, make sure you spell the web address exactly as it's just been given – if you substitute a 'z' for an 's', you'll end up at another site.

Kids Health http://www.kidshealth.org. This American site has sections for kids and teens as well as parents, and has loads of useful information about general health, fitness and nutrition, and specific illnesses.

National Autism Society http://www.oneworld.org/autism_uk. You'll find information about autism and Asperger syndrome here, along with details of NAS events and services.

The National Meningitis Trust http://www.meningitis-trust.org.uk. This clearly designed site sets out to offer 'research, education and support'. You'll find emergency information here, along with details of the meningitis immunization programme.

Net Doctor http://www.netdoctor.co.uk. You can find lots of useful information about medical problems at this clear and responsible site, along with interactive 'Ask the Doctor' features and discussion groups.

NHS Direct http://www.nhsdirect.nhs.uk. The NHS's own 'gateway to health information on the net', this has guides to treating common symptoms at home, links to loads of useful sites and lots more.

Patient UK http://www.patient.co.uk. A British directory of health-related websites, this site is run by two GPs and is clear and easy to use.

Royal National Institute for the Blind http://www.rnib.org.uk. This site has news, features, a discussion board and a useful general web directory too.

Talk Eczema http://www.talkeczema.com/. A clear and coherent site offering advice and support for eczema sufferers and their families.

Shopping

Sometimes, when you've got kids, you just can't get out to the shops. Consequently, all parents know how valuable mail order is. The net takes mail order into another dimension. It makes a huge range of products available to you, and it lets you shop from home, when it suits you. The following section contains some of the better child/parent-related net shops. But there are loads more online. For more shopping links, try Shopsmart **http://www.shopsmart.com** or the *Guardian*'s own Shopping site **http://www.guardian.co.uk/shopping**.

Amazon **http://www.amazon.co.uk**. Still the best online shop – get books, music, videos and DVDs, video games, software, toys and much more.

Babies "R" Us **http://www.babiesrus.co.uk**. A Toys "R" Us site aimed at babies, this doesn't just sell toys but has all sorts of other baby-related products as well.

Boden **http://www.boden.co.uk**. The website of the well-known clothes catalogue, this has sections on kids and babies.

Dawson and Son **http://www.dawson-and-son.com**. A wonderful site selling the kinds of lovingly crafted wooden toys parents love.

Early Learning Centre **http://www.elc.co.uk**. If you're one of the few parents in the UK who doesn't get sent the toy catalogue in the mail, check in here for a mainstream but dependable selection of toys.

Ebay **http://www.ebay.com**. If you can't find a toy in the shops, this huge American auction site might come to your aid, though you have to plan ahead if you buy from a seller in the States.

Great Little Trading Company **http://www.gltc.co.uk**. The online companion to the print catalogue, this sells a huge range of kid-related products, from bed-linen to toys.

JoJo Maman Bebe **http://www.jojomamanbebe.co.uk**. Get maternity wear, baby clothes, toys and more at this clearly designed site.

Just for Fun http://www.justforfun.co.uk/. A clear user-friendly online shop specializing in party goods – fancy dress, tableware, party packs etc.

Learning Store http://www.learningstore.co.uk. A shopping site that specializes in educational software, with over 1200 titles on offer, apparently.

Letterbox http://www.l-box.co.uk. A good place to visit if you're looking for an alternative to the big toy brands – get dressing-up stuff, wooden toys and lots more here.

Moonpig http://www.moonpig.com. If you have a birthday card emergency and you can't get out of the house, you can order a personalized card here and get it posted.

Mothercare http://www.mothercare.com. The well-known high street chain's website sells its range of baby/child-related products and also hosts community/information areas for parents.

Party Box http://www.partybox.co.uk/. You can buy masks, pinatas and games, and choose between thirty different themes (from 'Alien Encounter' to 'Mystical Unicorn') for kids' parties at this useful site.

The Party Store http://www.thepartystore.co.uk. One of the best of the online party stores, this has a great selection of themed party supplies (pirates, *Bob the Builder*), balloons and fancy dress.

Toys "R" Us http://www.toysrus.co.uk. The website of the big toy chain doesn't quite have the range of its real world mega-stores, but it's still useful, if rather mainstream.

Tridias http://www.tridias.co.uk/. Another well-known mail order catalogue that has moved online, this has a nice, offbeat selection of toys. The party section is excellent.

Urchin http://www.urchin.co.uk. One for the design-conscious parents, this site sells a wide range of kid-related product, from car seats and buggies to toys and bedroom furniture.

Find out more
about the net

The idea behind this book has been to help you learn about the net, so that you can help your kids get the most out of it. For obvious reasons, the bulk of the book has been given over to practical advice. However, the net isn't just a useful tool. It's an interesting subject in its own right. If you or your children want to find out more about the net, how it was developed, how it might change in the future, here are a few books you might find useful:

A Brief History of the Future by John Naughton (Phoenix Press). Probably the most accessible and interesting history of the net so far, from the Observer's online specialist. Find out more at **http://www.briefhistory.com**.

From Anarchy to Power by Wendy M. Grossman (NYU Press). Subtitled 'The Net Comes of Age', this has detailed accounts of recent net history, from virus scares to battles over encryption. A follow-up to *net.wars*, Grossman's excellent account of the net's early days. There's some additional material online at **http://www.nyupress.nyu.edu/fap**.

The Future Just Happened by Michael Lewis (Hodder and Stoughton). As mentioned before, this attempt to look at the net's cultural impact has a few too many sweeping generalizations, but lots of great reporting about recent net events. The tie-in website is good too **http://news.bbc.co.uk/hi/english/static/in_depth/programmes/2001/future/default.stm**.

The Hacker Ethic by Pekka Himanen (Vintage) A rather idealistic essay about the way hacker attitudes to information and other things might influence culture in general – a good present for smart computer-mad teens. You can do some more research and talk to like minds at **http://www.hackerethic.org**.

The Parent's Guide to Protecting Your Children in Cyberspace by Parry Aftab (McGraw Hill). The book you are currently reading sets out to tell you what you need to know about keeping your children safe. But if you want more detail, albeit with a mainly American focus, Parry Aftab's book is very useful. You'll find information relating to the book at **http://www.cyberangels.org**.

Pocket Internet (Economist Books). Basically a book-length glossary of computer/net related terms – with the emphasis on e-commerce, but still very useful.

The Victorian Internet by Tom Standage (Phoenix Press). A very readable attempt to undercut the techno-hype surrounding the web, by comparing it to the cultural fuss generated in the nineteenth century by the advent of the telegraph. The author's homepage is definitely worth a look **http://www.tomstandage.com**.

Weaving the Web by Tim Berners-Lee (Texere Publishing) The man who developed the web tells you how he did it and what he hopes will happen next. His homepage is at **http://www.w3.org/People/Berners-Lee/**.

Of course, if you want to find out what's currently happening online, the best place to go is the net itself. There are now lots of websites that specialize in net news – everything from breaking stories to more in-depth analysis of ongoing trends and developments. Here are a few worth investigating:

BBC News **http://news.bbc.co.uk**. As a whole, the Beeb's news site is as good as you'd expect. The net-related news is usually in the Sci/Tech section.

C/Net **http://www.news.com**. A huge site, covering computers, the net and much more, C/Net boasts that it runs 'tech news first' and it's true that it has become the first port of call if you want to know what's going on in the mainstream net world.

The *Guardian* Net News **http://www.guardian.co.uk/netnews**. There's a special area on the general *Guardian* site devoted to the latest net stories. You'll also find useful guides to current hot issues like the Microsoft break-up.

The Register **http://www.theregister.co.uk**. In contrast to the press-release journalism you find on many technology news sites, this British effort manages to dig out some real stories and serves them up with a lot of homegrown attitude. Informative and amusing.

Salon **http://www.salon.com**. Salon set out to be a kind of *New Yorker* on the web and has struggled over the last year. But its net coverage, which focuses as much on culture as business, is consistently excellent (and much ripped-off).

Tasty Bits from the Technology Front **http://www.tbtf.com**. The website of a much-praised weekly mail-out of technology/net news – check in here to subscribe and to catch up on past issues.

Wired News **http://www.wired.com**. This started out as one of the online extensions of the well-known print magazine. Now those connections are gone, but it remains a very useful site, covering the culture and business of new technology.

ZDNet UK **http://www.zdnet.co.uk**. The online home of the UK end of the big American computer magazine publishers, this has loads of net-related news, plus other information aggregated from the print magazines (e.g. computer buying guides and the like).

Internet Service Poviders

There are hundreds of companies offering to sell you internet access, some big, some small, and some you may never have heard of before. What follows is a quick list of some of the better-known operations, with contact details. A word of warning – the ISP business is still rather fluid. For a more up-to-date and comprehensive list, try the web or the monthly net magazines. *Internet Magazine* has some good webpages on ISPs at **http://www.internet-magazine.com/isp/index.asp**. The paper version of the magazine runs monthly ISP reviews and is definitely worth a look at too, especially the table which rates the ISPs' performances over the last half-year. Alternatively, try ISP Review **http://www.ispreview.co.uk/** for more ISP news and reviews.

AOL – 0800 376 5432 **http://www.aol.co.uk**

Beeb.net – 0808 100 4950 **http://www.beeb.net/**

BT Internet/Openworld – 0800 800001 **http://www.btopenworld.com**

ClaraNet – 0207 903 3000 **http://www.clara.net**

Compuserve – 0870 6000 800 **http://www.compuserve.co.uk**

Connect Free – 0870 742 1111 **http://www.connectfree.co.uk**

Demon – 0800 027 9200 **http://www.demon.net**

Easynet Dial – 0800 053 0551 **http://www.easynet.co.uk**

FreeNetName 0870 909 0586 **http://www.freenetname.co.uk**

Freeserve – 0870 872 0099 **http://www.freeserve.net**

Free UK – 0845 355 5555 **http://www.freeuk.com/**

Frontier Internet Services – 0845 601 1279 **http://www.frontier.net.uk/**

Global Internet – 0870 909 8041 **http://www.global.net.uk**

IC24 – 0870 909 0925 **http://www.ic24.net**

Madasafish – 08707 45 48 28 **http://www.madasafish.com**

MSN UK – 08457 002000 **http://www.msn.co.uk**

Netscape Online – 0800 923 0009 http://www.netscapeonline.co.uk

NowNet – 0870 600 6667 http://www.nownet.co.uk

NTL – 0800 052 1815 http://www.ntl.co.uk

Onyx – 0345 715715 http://www.onyxnet.co.uk

Pipex – 0870 600 4454 http://www.pipex.com/

Telewest – 0800 953 5383 http://www.telewest.co.uk

Tiscali – 0845 66 0 1010 http://www.tiscali.co.uk

UK Online – 0800 053 4500 http://www.ukonline.co.uk/

U-Net – 0845 330 8000 http://www.u-net.net

Virgin.net – 0845 650 0000 http://www.virgin.net/

Which? Online – 0845 983 0240 http://www.which.net/

Glossary

I've tried to keep techno-jargon to a minimum in this book.
However, when you're writing about the net, it's hard
to eliminate it completely. What follows is a brief glossary
that should come in handy if you get stuck. It certainly
isn't comprehensive. If you need a longer dictionary
of techno-speak, the best place to go is online. Here
are a few web-based glossaries worth consulting:

The Jargon File **http://www.jargon.org**
NetLingo **http://www.netlingo.com**
PC Webopaedia **http://www.pcwebopedia.com**
What Is **http://www.whatis.com**

A

ActiveX Control ActiveX is a programming language used to deliver multimedia via the web. A control is Microsoft's version of the plug-in, something you add to your browser so that it can handle a particular type of web multimedia.

ADSL Asymmetric Digital Subscriber Line. This uses normal copper telephone lines to deliver a high-speed connection to the net.

Anonymous FTP The procedure which lets you access FTP sites and download files without having to give your real name/address.

Applet A small program written in Java which can be placed on a webpage.

ASCII American Standard Code for Information Exchange: the set of standard unformatted characters and numbers – plain text, in other words – that all computers can understand.

Attachments Files, graphics, pictures, sounds, even programs that are attached to email messages and sent across the net.

B

Bandwidth Network capacity: the amount of data that can be sent over a net connection.

Betas Test versions of software currently in development and due for eventual commercial release.

Binary File A non-text file: everything from sound and images to compressed archives.

Bits Used to denote units of data and not to be confused with bytes. One byte consists of eight bits (each either a 1 or a 0). Bits are the measurement used when talking about data transmission speeds – as in 56 kilobit modems. Bytes are used when talking about memory and disk space – as in a 4 gigabyte hard disk.

Bot A software robot – i.e. an automated, autonomous program which performs a particular task online.

Bookmarks A list of the addresses of your favourite websites set up to allow you to access them a little bit quicker. Microsoft calls these Favourites.

Bounced Mail Email that doesn't reach its destination and is returned to the sender with an error message.

Bps Bits per second.

Broadband Strictly speaking, a form of data transmission in which a single medium (for example, a wire) can carry several channels at once. More generally, broadband is used to refer to fast connections capable of carrying large amounts of data at high speeds.

Browser The software program you use to move around the web and download and view pages.

Bug An error/defect in a software program that causes that program to crash or not work properly.

....

C
....

Cache The place where your browser stores all the files (pages and pictures) it downloads from the web.

CD-ROM Compact Disc-Read-Only Memory: a kind of optical disk that can store large amounts of information – typically these are used for big software programs, games, sound and video.

CD-RW Compact Disc-ReWritable disk: a type of CD disk that you can write on to as well as play. A CD-RW drive can play CD-ROMs as well as write on to CD-R disks.

Chat Online conversations in which participants exchange text in real time.

Chatroom An online space where you can chat with a group of users.

Client/Server Servers are central computers on which data is stored. Clients are the software programs that access data stored on a server. More generally, client means any bit of software that accesses information via a network.

Compressed Archive One file that contains several other files that have been compressed to make them quicker to send around the net.

Content The stuff on the website that you actually read, look at or play.

Cookie A little identifying text file placed on your computer by a website. When you go back to that site, it reads the cookie to tell what you did there before and adds more information.

Cross-posting The practice of sending messages or posts to several discussion groups at once.

Cybercafé A café complete with net-connected terminals.

Cyberspace The place you're in when you're on the net – a term first coined by SF writer William Gibson.

Cybersquatting The practice of buying up internet domain names (often using well-known company names) with a view to selling them on to the 'rightful owner'.

....

D

....

Default The standard setting that a device or a piece of software automatically selects unless you specify something different.

Domain Name System Also referred to as the DNS. The net's system of addresses, in which each computer on the net has a unique IP number and domain name.

Download If you transfer a file from a computer on the net on to your PC, you're downloading it.

DVD Digital Versatile Disc / Digital Video Disc: a new type of CD-ROM capable of storing much more information than old-style CD-ROMs.

....

E

....

E-commerce All-purpose term for any kind of business effort online.

Email Electronic Mail. Messages sent via the net.

Emoticons Also known as smileys. Little faces made up of text, intended to add emotion / tone to online communications and hence reduce the potential for misunderstanding.

Encryption A way of encoding online communications and hence keeping them private.

Extension As in File Extension. A group of letters, which come after the file name and identify what type of file it is.

....

F

....

FAQ Frequently Asked Questions: a file of answers to standard queries.

Filter Software designed to block access to certain sites – either those that the maker of the program deems unacceptable or sites specified by the user.

Flame Abusive / insulting online message often fired off in anger at some mistake or perceived slight.

Frames A method of splitting webpages up into separate windows.

Freeware Software you don't have to pay for, or, if you believe the purists, software you can modify because the source code is open and available.

FTP File Transfer Protocol: this lets you upload or download files to and from the net.

G

GIF Graphic Interchange Format: one of the most popular formats for putting images on the web, this is typically used for graphics.

Gigabyte One gigabyte is equal to 1,024 megabytes, which is a lot of bytes – currently the standard way of measuring the size of hard drives.

Graphics card A board that plugs into a personal computer to boost its display capabilities.

GUI Graphical User Interface: GUIs make computers user-friendly by replacing text commands with a visual interface made up of cursors and icons.

H

Hard disk A magnetic disk in your PC, on which you store data. Hard disks hold more data and are faster than floppy disks.

Hackers Originally this meant someone who loved programming and messing around with computers. People who identify with this dismiss younger hackers who get into headline-grabbing mischief as 'crackers'.

Header The basic details about the message – what it's about, who sent it and when.

Helper Apps Helper Applications. Programs that can handle some of the multimedia content you find on the web.

Hierarchies The thematic categories used to distinguish different Usenet newsgroups – i.e. the little suffixes that appear at the start of the group name – as in rec.football or alt.flame.

Homepage A homepage can be (a) the first page your browser shows when it starts; or (b) the first page of a website. But most non-geeky types now think of a homepage as a personal website put up by an ordinary net user.

Host Another word for a computer connected to the Internet.

HTML HyperText Markup Language: the computer code used to create webpages.

HTML Mail Email that doesn't come in the form of plain text but is formatted using HTML.

HTTP HyperText Transfer Protocol: the protocol which enables communications on the web.

Hypertext A method of formatting computer text so that documents are linked to each other.

....

I

....

Image map A large graphic image that contains links to other pages.

Instant Messages Short messages sent to friends who are on the net, usually with a view to setting up a real-time chat.

Interface The thing that comes between you and all the zeros and ones sitting on your computer (i.e. icons, folders and so on) and helps you actually use your machine.

Internet Service Provider A company that provides access to the net.

IP (Internet Protocol) address A collection of four numbers, separated by full stops/periods (e.g. 123.4.56.891).

IRC Internet Relay Chat: a method for chatting in real time on the net.

ISDN Integrated Services Digital Network: ISDN lines offer reasonably fast connections to the net and can carry voice calls at the same time.

J

Java/Javascript Programming languages that can be used to create interactive multimedia effects on the web.

JPEG Joint Photographic Experts Group: a way of compressing and formatting photographs so that they can be displayed on the web.

L

Link A connection between one web document and another. Click on it and you move to the linked page.

Lurkers Net slang for those who hang around in newsgroups (and chatrooms), read what other people say but don't actually post anything themselves.

M

Mailbomb An attempt to crash a particular system by sending it a huge amount of email.

Many-to-many network One way of describing the net, which lets lots of people receive and transmit messages – unlike the TV network, which is one-to-many.

Meta Tags A way of marking a particular webpage, so that search engines can more easily identify and log its content.

MHz Short for Megahertz. One MHz equals one million cycles per second. Microprocessor speed is measured in megahertz – a microprocessor that runs at 200 MHz executes 200 million cycles per second.

Microprocessor/Processor The brains of your PC, this is where it does its calculating and is sometimes referred to as the central processor or the CPU.

MIME Multipurpose Internet Mail Extensions: the standard used to handle attachments to electronic messages.

Mirror Site A copy of a website that is situated on another computer in another location.

Modem A modem converts the digital information your computer works with into audio signals that can be sent down a standard telephone line.

MPEG Moving Picture Expert Group: the standard for compressing audio and video so that they can be sent more easily across the net.

MP3 The letters are a shortened version of MPEG Layer 3, a technique used to compress music files to about a tenth of their normal size, without much loss of overall sound quality.

MUD Multiple User Dungeons (or Dimensions or Dialogues): chat spaces in which users have collectively talked up a whole world, with its own rules and customs.

Multimedia Basically a combination of different media forms (text, sound, video) in one integrated, interactive whole.

N

Netiquette The net's code of conduct.

Newbie Slang term for someone new to the net.

Newsgroups Online forums where people discuss a variety of subjects.

NNTP Network News Transfer Protocol: the protocol used to handle messages to and from newsgroups.

O

Offline Browsing Reading webpages you've previously downloaded while offline.

Online Service An business that, along with net access, also sells special content, chatrooms, conferences and other services.

Operating System The basic software running on your computer, the program that lets you use all the other programs (or applications). Most computers run Windows 95/98. Other operating systems include Unix, DOS and Linux.

P

Patch A small chunk of code designed to fix a bug in a larger program.

Plug-ins Programs you add to a browser, so it can handle different sorts of files, specifically multimedia files.

Point of Presence The place, or rather telephone number, you dial to connect to your ISP.

POP3 As in POP3 mail. The letters and number stand for Post Office Protocol, version 3. This is the protocol that is used when receiving email.

Portal Websites that contain all the services people are most likely to use online – free email, chatrooms, conferences, homepage facilities, online shopping, search engines, directories and much else.

Post A message sent to a discussion group.

PPP Point to Point Protocol: the protocol used to hook computers up to the net.

Protocol A shared language used by computers so that they can communicate with other computers.

....

R

....

RAM Random Access Memory: best thought of as your computer's short-term memory, this helps make your programs run more smoothly.

....

S

....

Search Engine Programs that let net users search for pages containing particular words.

Shareware Software you can try before actually buying it. Shareware programs are made available for free, but lack certain features or will 'time out' after a month.

Sig File As in 'signature file'. A combination of name, address, contact details, amusing quotations and even ascii art which is attached to email as a way of personalizing it.

SLIP Serial Line Internet Protocol: the protocol that allows access to the net via a telephone line and a modem. Outdated now and replaced by PPP.

Smiley see Emoticons, above.

SMTP Simple Mail Transfer Protocol: the protocol used to send email.

Source The underlying version of a particular web document, a version which contains all the HTML tags which make the page look the way it does.

Spam Net slang for unsolicited junk email sent in bulk to thousands of users at once.

Standard A format approved and accepted by the computer industry as a whole.

Streaming As in 'streaming video'. Video or audio files that you can play as you download them from the web.

Surfing All-purpose term used to make the business of accessing the net seem more exciting than it usually is.

T

TCP/IP TCP stands for Transmission Control Protocol. IP stands for Internet Protocol. Both 'protocols' allow your computer to communicate with the Internet.

TCP/IP Stack A TCP/IP stack is several bits of software in one – TCP/IP software, packet driver software and sockets software – each of which is needed in order to send and receive data across the net.

Thread An ongoing conversation taking place in a discussion group or mailing list.

TLA Three-Letter Acronyms: conversational shorthand (BTW equals 'by the way') used to compress electronic messages.

U

Upload The opposite of download – i.e. transferring a file from your computer to another computer in a different location.

URL Uniform Resource Locator: the address given to computers/files on the web.

USB Universal Serial Bus: essentially, a new standard for connecting peripheral devices to a computer. Most USB devices are designed to run off your PC's power source, so you don't need to plug them in to the mains.

Usenet The name for the network of newsgroups.

Uuencode A way of encoding binary files (e.g. images) so that they can be attached to email and sent across the net. This is gradually being replaced by MIME.

....

V

....

Virus A malicious program, usually hidden inside another program. When you run the main program, the virus is activated too and can damage your computer.

....

W

....

WAP Wireless Application Protocol: this allows you to access information over a network via handheld wireless devices (e.g. mobile phones) and personal digital assistants (e.g. the Palm Pilot).

World Wide Web The graphical multimedia portion of the Internet.

Weblog A page of links to other content, usually updated on a regular basis. Usually the work of one person.

Webmaster The person who runs a particular website (i.e. keeps it working and updated). The webmaster can be the designer of the page, but not necessarily.

Webpage A document, usually formatted in HTML, which might contain text, images, animations, sound and even video.

Web Ring Loose collectives of sites all devoted to the same basic subject.

Website A collection of pages put up by an individual, institution or business.

Index

Acknowledgements

Thanks to Mathew Clayton of the *Guardian* for supporting the idea to do this book from way back when. Thanks also to my agent, Cat Ledger, for fighting my corner with her usual skill. Thank you to both Toby Mundy and Alice Hunt of Atlantic Books who came up with all sorts of clever ideas that made the book you hold in your hands much better than it might have been if it had just been left to me. Alice's organizational skills and general patience also helped me get the thing finished on time. I also owe a serious debt of gratitude to the book's copy-editor, Neil Foxlee. Neil not only sorted out my copious grammatical errors and spelling mistakes but also contributed lots of useful suggestions and put up with my general slowness when it came to finishing the book. Cheers, Neil. Finally, thanks to Bryony Newhouse for making the book look so good.

Parts of the book may have appeared in a slightly different form in some of my journalism. Thanks to the various editors who have put up with my deadline surfing over the years, in particular Vic Keegan, Neil McIntosh and Jack Schofield of the *Guardian*. Friends and family offered support and advice whilst I was writing this guide. Thanks to everyone – you know who you are. Thanks in particular to my mum Helen, to my brothers Jon and Rob, to Maddie, to Peter, Phill, Jonathan and Lydia, John and Corinne and Pat and Geoff. Writing this book meant I spent less time with my kids over the summer than might otherwise have been the case. Sorry, Lee, Cameron and Rowan, and thanks for putting up with me. Finally, thanks to Kim. Once again, I would never have got this finished without you.